A Mind's Eye View

A Mind's Eye View

Marie Thompson

Library of Congress Control Number:		2019901088
ISBN:	Hardcover	978-1-7960-1318-4
	Softcover	978-1-7960-1317-7
	eBook	978-1-7960-1316-0

Print information available on the last page.

Rev. date: 05/22/2019

To order additional copies of this book, contact:
Xlibris
1-888-795-4274
www.Xlibris.com
Orders@Xlibris.com
769686

HAMLET: *My father! Me thinks I see my father.*
HORATIO: *Where, my lord?*
HAMLET: *In my mind's eye, Horatio.*

Hamlet, by William Shakespeare, 1602

CONTENTS

Essays

Poetry

Short Stories

And…for fun…

Essays

ADVANTAGES OF DISORDER

Don't you hate it when someone suggests you should organize your chaos? Such arrogance! What *they* consider a mess is actually meticulously organized. The piles of paper in my office may look thrown together, but there is order that others just don't recognize. I like my befuddled world. It suits me. My sister has a room where she dumps everything she doesn't know what to do with, and one glance could imply psychosis. There is no clue to what might be within the Pyrenean Mountain peaks of plastic store bags, and new ones continue to join the *Forgotten* residing within those pinnacles. The sense of discovery would be completely missed if she used the closets. Where is the satisfaction in that?

There are those who believe disorder is anarchy and argue in support of their opinion. I would argue for the advantages, believing disorder is in the eyes of the beholder. Firstly, one is ensured of privacy. No one would dare probe through my seemingly slipshod filing system, and my sister's room guarantees it remains her own terrain. Secondly, a major advantage of disorder is it creates energy. If one is of the type who cannot happily reside in disarray, the resulting angst can produce determination, inventiveness, and an orderly environment. Rampaging mob energy has been known to take down a dictatorship and bring hope for a new future. Unremarkable lines drawn on paper by a young child can become communicative symbols through casual yet unwavering manipulation. There are occasions when even my own jumbled contemplations can give me a headache until the triumph of acuity is sweated out.

A montage of pieces of material placed on a single surface can, at first glance, cause confusion and the viewer could walk on. A second glance, however, may allow insight to discipline and order and, yes, beauty. The Los Angeles' Walt Disney Concert Hall is free-form beauty to some, while others think Gehry's exterior design of stainless steel concave sections are a confused monstrosity. What about all those crispy golden leaves under foot each autumn that get whipped by the wind and scattered? As they break down, blankets of cornflake-sized pieces spread, and mess up the land. But there is organization here too—Nature's plan will turn disorder into future life.

Let me take my position a little farther. Disorders in the deoxyribonucleic acid (DNA) are changes to the base pair sequence of the genetic material of an organism. Mutations can be caused by errors in the genetic material during cell division, resulting in variations in the gene pool. Such disorder can, on occasion, result in miracles. As an example, a butterfly may produce an offspring with a new mutation that changes its colour and makes it more difficult for predators to see. This change is, of course, an advantage; the mutation may survive and, over time, this particular genus may show up as a larger percentage of the future butterfly population, ensuring its survival.

There are those who argue the negatives of disorder, and I concede there are some, but many like a befuddled world. I feel empowered when I lay hands on an item without the assistance of a detective, although I admit there could be a squashed sticky crumb or two attached. Perhaps my argument in favour of disorder will not pose a convincing defence against those intolerants who translate disorder to a harsh definition; however, it is worth remembering there can be diverse interpretations of a word. As with many beliefs, persuasion and flexibility can play a role, and I would include humour. I'm happy in a lackadaisical lifestyle; my sister is too. In the wise words of Paul McCartney, let it be; let *us* be. Please.

A SIGNIFICANT READING

A book that gave me immense pleasure when I was about ten years old was Gavin Maxwell's Ring of Bright Water. The story revolves around a couple of sea otters that were brought by Maxwell from Iraq to Camusfearna, his private paradise in the remote Scottish Highlands. His detailed descriptions of the otters' comical antics, the stark beauty of the rugged land, and the day-to-day survival in that isolated area, introduced me to the wonders of nature as no other reading at that time. I became aware of the pleasures that solitude could offer—a non-existent experience in my crowded, rambunctious home. My eyes danced on the words as I eagerly turned page after page, eventually reaching the closing sentence. There were many new books that followed, but the deep respect I feel for the "blue marble" we call home, began all those years ago.

I attended a prominent church for a couple of years before I felt challenged by its doctrine and sermons that certainly contained the words of love and forgiveness, but eventually I found myself at a crossroad. A close friend and an active member of the ministry decided to also leave the church at that time, and become a student of A Course in Miracles. Eventually, he became an enthusiastic follower. After several conversations with him and others involved with these new studies, I decided to attend a few workshops, and then joined a study group.

A Course in Miracles, published by the Foundation for Inner Peace, is Christian in principle, and deals with universal spiritual themes. Emphasis is made that it is but one version of the universal curriculum, that nothing real can be threatened, nothing unreal exists, and that truth can be unrecognized but not be changed. Accepting that love and forgiveness is our true nature is an ever-present challenge to me because I seem to have my feet firmly on the path where the ego dominates. The choice would appear to be easy, but I have found much confusion and continue searching for clarity.

My study of the Course has been on and off over the years. My footsteps have wavered, but in spite of my confusion, I have begun to see differently, deeper—beyond the obvious. My heart is more open; I'm less judgmental and more conscious of this moment—the Now. Eckhart Tolle's book, The Power of Now, stresses avoiding thoughts of the past or future but I am far from that coup. I am relaxed around sickness because it is incidental to the person who takes my attention, although sorrow sometimes catches up with me on the way home from the hospitals where I volunteer. When I initially became involved with these studies, I felt adrift and uneasy. The simple message was incomprehensible to me because it seemed to say everything I relied on thus far was unreal. I felt my spiritual base crumble under the weight of trying to rethink through misunderstanding and old beliefs. The responsibility for *the world I see is the world I create* needed to be faced. Is this world that I find so full of wonder my fantasy controlled by my ego? Did Gavin Maxwell share in the same illusion when he described the distinct colours and textures of lichens clinging to weathered rocks or the silver light on the water where lithe elongated creatures played? What about those who work to better the world, to clean the air, to save a species on the brink of extinction, or face the challenges of healing the sick? For that matter, those who work to destroy and corrupt? These many questions seem only to multiply and few have been answered, yet I continue my search for understanding.

A scientist colleague published a book corroborating that every individual specimen is uniquely different; each leaf on the same plant has distinct qualities, each ant has its own exclusive feature. Such discovery captivates me but I am challenged to reconcile this emotion to the Course's teaching that this world is unreal. The reverence I feel over the great beauty and breath-taking marvels around me continues and I often feel connected to the point I am absorbed by it. I am aware the wrenching stories reported daily in the media are in juxtaposition to that elation, and they add extra discord to my confused position. When my eyes and heart are open, I project sensitivity and love, and my encounters return the same to me. Is this experience perhaps a holy encounter, a reflection of God's perfection within all of us and is a part of my "real" world after all? I feel quietude as I ponder such a question. It is only one of many. There are moments when I feel on the brink of clarity, but that vanishes with a blink of an eye. I trust I will get "it" eventually.

BE CAREFUL WHAT YOU SAY

Isn't it amazing how oo, ahh and ee, joined with other sounds, have somehow evolved to become a means to communicate in the distinctive human manner? Incredibly, air passing through the cavity of the larynx causes two folds of mucous membranes projecting there to vibrate. The resulting vocal sounds eventually produced language. Such an evolution is staggering. A series of grunts slowly, methodically, developed to a level so sophisticated that particular sounds strung like beads on a thread produced recognized words that expressed universal joy, sadness, intellect, anger, fear and love. Emotions and language are bound one to the other. A memory associated with a word can be powerfully influential. Interpretations of certain words are often prejudiced by an individual's life experiences. The tone of the voice adds emphasis to what is being relayed. A lilt, a drop in tone or a click of the tongue can give entirely different meanings to a word although the route sounds are identical. Adding more confusion, a single word often has need of clarification. *Will* could mean a legal document, a man's name, or self-control.

All languages seem to have pitfalls, whether it is one's own or that of another country. When listening to an American speak I often have difficulty in differentiating between *can* and *can't*. To my British trained ear, they sound the same, and if I don't get it right, my interpretation can place the speaker in the opposite position desired and embarrass us both. My ear is becoming more sensitive, fortunately, and I think my clipped English enunciation is softer and easier on others' ears, but there is something to be said for Henry Higgins' lament: *Oh, why can't the English set a good example to people whose English is painful to your ears?*

Certain words are held in high regard. *Truth* is a word on which ethics and integrity stand but it can be manipulated. Realistically, there are times when one compromises truth when the intent behind the word must be considered. When a rather rounded friend looks like a tomato in a certain red dress, I believe it is acceptable to join truth with kindness and diplomacy to prevent her potential humiliation. Is it manipulation? Yes—possibly ego too. And then there is *trust* which, to my mind, equates to *hope*. There is a tendency to trust persons to be truthful who hold a high office. Their speeches, however, are often the work of professional writers who are skilled in influencing a bias in favour of the speaker. One can trust/hope this applies to very few officials.

The phrase "I give you my word" is uncompromising and immensely honourable but rarely heard now. An added handshake enforced an understanding or agreement. Nowadays, we are bound by the complicated written language within extensive legal documents that confuse, and wheel and deal. Regretfully, it appears a man can seldom stand behind his word because he cannot; the stakes are too high. However, in my world, you do need to be careful what you say. If you give me your word I will be counting on it. And you? Rest assured, you can count on mine. When we shake hands, it is unbreakable.

CARR PARK aka MY PLACE

I have a place—a special place, where I magically escape into another world and become spiritually uplifted. I go there as often as possible. It is called Carr Park. This small oasis offers time out from pastel stucco and traffic emissions. Cluttered thoughts are calmed and I allow serenity to take over and ease emotions and questions that sometimes weigh me down. There was a time when I drove passed without a second glance; my mind too busy to notice what was being offered. Then, on impulse a few months ago, I parked on the roadside, took off my sandals, and entered a pocket of timelessness. About five acres, the park has a densely vegetated island surrounded by a moat of murky water. The remaining land is grass covered, and heavy leafed eucalyptus, willow and maple sway in ocean breezes that perform Nature's music. The ducks and birds were just a part of the scene at first, but soon I became aware of not only the beauty of each species but also the uniqueness of each individual. Insentience, I became a bird watcher or, more precisely, a waterfowl watcher. Thanks to the local flea market, I accrued a couple of reference books, and now a pair of binoculars which I hold at the ready to identify shapes, colours and group behaviours. I am gradually learning to distinguish subtle differences, and each visit brings discovery. I recognize individuals with characteristics I've personified. A plump Ross goose has a damaged left wing so flight feathers stand upright in a perpetual high-five; it has adapted and is healthy and feeding well. Frequently the blue heron that I have named Ardi after his family name of Ardeidae, stands silently in the under-growth of the island. He is about four feet tall on long skinny legs, and is most impressive with a sinuous neck and a thick, dagger-like bill that spears a fish or other tasty treat with a rapid thrust. Today, he appears to be mulling over the antics of half a dozen white billed coots whose heads pump back and forth as they progress across the water. Their bizarre feet with oversized greenish-yellow toes that allow walking on water as well as land, churn a crust of leaves, bread and plastic. To my right are regular long-term vacationers—black-necked Canada geese who are fixed on ransacking the banks for prime greens. They look comical with shreds of grass hanging from their polished bills.

From the embankment, I watch a brown pelican with its six foot wingspan circle the lake several times. With its great head resting back against sturdy shoulders, it makes a final turn to position itself for a landing. Yellow webs stretched wide, it skis on the surface of the water before coming to a smooth finish with those giant wings tucked tight to its sides. The resulting wake unsettles the water that is syrupy with silt and flotillas of trash. A female mallard with metallic blue wing flashes seems unperturbed, even though she is in command of newly hatched ducklings taking a swim. Light baths the iridescent green of the drake's head to announce his whereabouts as sentinel.

Of course, this park is not my personal property but a sense of ownership came early. I slowly navigate around the lake, monitoring conditions of the water, collecting too much trash and side stepping a thick layer of slimy guano. Smiles are exchanged with others, our few words softened by a calm countenance. Excited voices from the children's playground in the distance edge in, but they are a cheerful intrusion. Yesterday, they drew my attention to two Brandt cormorants poised in the eucalyptus to my right, and there, over on the island, several white egrets balanced on the tops of oak trees.

My visit now over for the day, I reluctantly walk to my car. Several stocky white geese waddle around my feet, honking for attention from yolk-yellow bills. I have nothing to offer, and they walk off in a huff like disgruntled madams. I laugh aloud at the theatrical spectacle. The car parked along-side mine discharges a family with bags of food scraps. An elderly man hauling a heavy sack of birdseed from a small truck waves to me. A quick eye and a piercing honk from the *ever watchful* is all it took to create the ensuing frenzied turbulence of ducks, geese and a couple of white swans to surround him. I watch in silence, rapt by the spectacle. The man's grin is wide as he calls out, wanting—needing—to express his delight. "Isn't it marvellous? I can't stay away."

DROUGHT

It doesn't look good...even with sporadic rainstorms and deep snowpack, California is in a continuing drought, and cherished defined seasons have become a fading reminiscence. Water conservation softens somewhat after an occasional celebrated winter, but it is soon imposed again.

Resistance to the labour intensive collecting of household "grey" water is a physical and emotional challenge. Saving the precious commodity is not easy. Shower heads do not cooperate by spraying directly into a bucket, and ensuring washing machine cycles empty anywhere but down a drain can lead to expletives heretofore unknown to man. I am, however, delighted I saved a few garden plants and have become more sensitive when handing a water filled bucket to a guest when they enter the sanctum of the bathroom.

California's rich colour palette changed to the soft hues of a desert—then to the savage reds of disaster. Tinder-dry brush or artificial synthetic fibre instantly turning into terrifying waves of flame and smouldering ash unifies annihilation with a filthy blanket of black and grey. Drought and fires destroy not only human townships but wildlife territory. Obliterated animal lairs and food sources force those surviving animals to overcome fear to forage for scraps amongst human trash. And they are welcomed.

Photosynthetic organisms produce the major amount of oxygen we need. Without trees and plant life there is no tool to clean the air through this system. Less green plants = less recycling of carbon dioxide = less oxygen production. Without adequate vegetation to soak up carbon dioxide, the increased air pollution irritates eyes, depletes energy, and debilitating allergies are increased dramatically. Robust new commercial and residential developments are putting enormous stress on the State's reduced resources and cause more people and more cars to vie for the same space. California is in trouble. It has to deal realistically with a multitude of complex challenges, of course, but safeguarding a healthy population must be part of the equation; particularly, as it is accepted California is now the beneficiary of China's polluted air too. The blue Pacific Ocean that laps our golden shores is deceiving. It looks picture perfect but dangerous pollutants still continue discharging from unscrupulous industries, and just below the sun-kissed surface are tons in staggering numbers of plastics that trap and kill the undeserving creatures of the deep.

Although this piece reflects my deep concern, I am lifted by hope because I am talking about the State of California, the place I call home. This State has a population of caring people who do what is necessary to meet a need, and its history proves it is so. Saving water is miserable, trying to keep cool in 90-100+ degree temperatures is miserable, sore eyes and sneezing is no fun either, but I join with all those others to do my part—for we are in this together, and together we can find a way to make our ailing home healthy again. Well, it is time for my shower. I have the bucket ready, and will make every effort to catch those precious droplets as they scatter around me. My garden will thank me, and I, in turn, thank all those who struggle along with me. Together we are the salve on this festering wound.

GARDENS

When I stop to breathe in the perfume of a flower in my garden, it is a reflective experience. One could say it is the pay-off for the on-going attention and sweat-labour demanded by my modest plot that communicates its thanks by producing a nascent tapestry. But there is more: the hypothesis becomes reality, bringing tranquillity and an invitation to become a scientist, an artist and environmentalist.

"A garden"—just two words that create a mental picture that is a juxtaposition of colour, texture and atmosphere, and is unilaterally understood because this single concept can be defined within a multitude of languages and backgrounds. Imagination has no limits, whether the creation is within a ceramic pot, a window box or stretched over several acres, but fidelity is required. Involvement with the land means work but it brings about a peace that is silent within, and rests the soul. The oriental garden arose from a spiritual base. Its complementary plant forms of varying texture and colour are restrained and subtle, and in harmony with water and stone. Home grown fruits and vegetables control what is put on the dining table, and a few sprigs of herbs give flavour when added to a recipe. Gertrude Stein's statement, "A rose is a rose is a rose," is now a cliché but can it be contradicted? There is no other way to compare such perfection than to itself. I concur, a rose **is.** We view physical beauty through the retina of the eye, but the image remains to be drawn upon at will through the "retina" of the brain—and is savoured. The pleasure, as repeated, causes the heart to slow and endorphins to rise.

An illusion? Perhaps? Nevertheless, the value of such an illusion is tangible.

In this increasingly crowded and artificial world, gardens take on added significance. Complete ecosystems within themselves, these oases clean the air, and provide habitat for insects and wildlife. Organic gardening is now practiced by many. Transitioning to this benign approach for food production is critical. The ground water has been put to great risk from excessive quantities of pesticides and chemical fertilizers used by the agriculture industry and American homeowners. Diane MacEashern in her book *Save Our Planet* explains there are 750 everyday ways we can help clean up the Earth. That's the personal reward. The planetary one is much greater. Gardeners can help restore the Earth in many simple ways. By favouring ivy or grass over concrete and asphalt, underground aquifers are allowed to replenish each time it rains. Every tree planted will help cool the earth by absorbing carbon dioxide—a major cause of global warming. Maintaining a green landscape also provides a haven for wildlife, especially needed now hundreds of thousands of birds are losing breeding grounds through deforestation.

An abundance of children's literature centres on the garden, and introduces the miracle of metamorphoses, hard-working beneficial bugs, and those who are dreaded enemies too. Author Frances Hodgson Burnett's book, *The Secret Garden,* took 230 pages to tell what all gardeners know: dilapidated ground can be transformed into something magical and positively affect the core of those involved with it. Perhaps "garden" is an allegory; for when nourished and tended, all life will flourish. Helping Nature thrive will satisfy long after the hoe is put back in the shed.

Impressionist Vincent van Gogh painted images of a small garden adjacent to the Saint-Paul de Mausole asylum where he lived for many years. Its trees and flowers brought him happiness and calmed his anxieties. Artist Claude Monet is as famous for his intensely loved garden in Giverny, as much as for his art. Hundreds of years ago, Flemish artists meticulously painted reproductions of flowers, fruits and insects to photographic quality and enables a particular specimen to be identified today.

Poet Wordsworth's words, "...my heart with pleasure fills, and dances with the daffodils," delights us with a cheerful image. Faulkner sharply defines the seasons in *The Marble Faun:* "We sit drinking tea beneath the lilacs on a summer afternoon. Across the sun-shot downs that smell like crispened warm fresh bread. My garden stark and white, ice bound and ghostly on the edge." Thoreau wrote, "True art is but the expression of our love of nature," and John Muir defended the conservation of the American wilderness. Contact with nature, either through a pair of binoculars, a pair of mud-caked work gloves or a cutting on the window sill, can bring about a softer heart and a determination to make it a better place for all of us. I am certainly trying to do that and am so grateful for the support and encouragement my garden gives me. The seasons are a timetable that ensures a perfect balance of rest and resurgence of life. I rest when the land rests, and don my gloves and sunhat when I feel an awakening under foot. My back and hands will get sore but I don't complain; the overwhelming gain is so worth it.

GOOD MORNING MOON

I walk early each morning, just as night slips quietly away, leaving a ghost-like landscape illuminated by opaque moonlight. I enjoy that time—there's a new day ahead. The waning moon hanging on in the new dawn sky has a "see you later" smile just for me. Over the past couple of weeks, each new day has been dragging its heels and I now step out into night left-overs. I walk accompanied by shadows at my side. I'm not complaining…the idea of a season change cheers me. The long days of summer have challenged with torturous high temperatures that sucked stunning landscape dry. I look forward to the return of green sweeping across the land that is waiting, open-mouthed—greedy for the predicted El Niño to arrive. With luck, perhaps we'll enjoy a winter cool too, and sparkling frost will crust rooftops and lawns again. Yes, the days are getting shorter but I don't mind a bit. My tank-top may evolve to a coat and muffler but I will continue with my early trek. You see, that moon and I have been together for some time now, and it is serious. I look up compulsively. No meteoroid slices the empyrean—only a "Red-Eye" hauling comatose space-travellers. The vast sky shimmers with stars held captive in the congested Heaven and they seem so close, like snow crystals ready to plummet on cue. With my mind's eye, I reach out and feel their frosty-thaw with my fingertips.

I can hardly move my neck from looking up at that ghostly sphere for so long, but it beckons to me and I cannot but pause in my step. As it fades into lucent space, I stiffly make my way home. The earth continues quietly on its axes and I am greeted by a blush of rose sweeping the Eastern horizon. Brave nocturnal cats, languid from the nip of night, stretch to motivate energy. I whisper, "good morning"; their backlit eyes follow me in silence. Flat silhouette shapes that floated unanchored earlier now emerge as textured flora. Abruptly, a single phrase by a vacationing Oregon Townsend's Warbler stirs the peace with his welcome to the new day. He is small but his bright yellow head and breast give him away high among the branches of a California pine. From the lacy leaves of several Jacaranda trees, a chorus of drowsy twitters protest the intrusion, then increases to a concerted frenzy.

Electric lights now leach from bathroom windows. In the distance a car engine roars. The day is no longer mine alone, and I hurriedly retreat. I turn into my driveway where an ornamental plum tree has become the pick-up arena for local sparrow-boys strutting their male egos. The foremost item of their concentration is the proliferation of their species, but they must be patient for the right time. The dainty females will eventually give in, perhaps just to stop their incessant chirping. It would sooth my irritated ear if a melody was sung to entice a romantic outcome, but I discovered they have no tolerance for my voice either.

I retreat to silence in the expanse of my back garden. I like to spend time looking through my telescope, even with its limited capacity. I dropped hints whenever a birthday or Christmas appeared on the horizon, but succumbed to the realization I have the power to control that myself, and am perusing models that correspond to my resources. As I gaze into the heavens, I become so engaged, my form seems to evaporate into the infinite expanse. The Moon, about one-fourth the size of the Earth in diameter, is an apparition now. I squint against the growing sunlight. I believe it was in 2010 when Dr. Thomas Watters of the Centre for Earth and Planetary Studies reported the Moon has shrunk over the past billion years but he assures we're not to worry; it is not going to disappear soon. As its interior cooled, the crust cracked and caused the surface to shrink on the scarps (cliffs) up to 100 meters high and a few kilometres long. That could indicate the Moon is still active.

There is much "out there". The mere thought of what I am missing makes my shoulders stoop. The fine telescope I covet, however, will soon be mine and I will look into that infinite expanse above and see things beyond what I can only imagine. I fill myself with excitement. In the meantime, I will continue to visit the Planetarium and get my stiff neck from there. Voices from dog walkers bring me back to the scene around me, but I don't mind. My private world will be mine again tomorrow; for a while anyway. I enter the house, and take my shoes off.

I BELIEVE IN ANGELS

The word angel originated from the Latin word angelus, meaning messenger. Artists have painted angels for centuries, but the earliest known work is a Christian image of Gabriel as an angel without wings in the Cubicolo dell'Annunziazione at the Catacomb of Priscilla, and dates to the middle of the third century. The earliest known image of angels *with* wings is on the "Prince's Sarcophagus", attributed to the time of Theodosius I (379–395), and discovered at Sarigüzel, near Istanbul, in the 1930s. There, angels wear elaborate shifts and golden cloaks, and have full-feathered wings. The Scriptures report angles are spiritual beings sent by God to be our guardians, and many mortals find comfort in the idea they have their own personal guardian angel whom they can name. I have one. I often felt a presence, and asked "it" to identify "itself". The name Michael came immediately to my mind, and I now draw comfort and companionship from him in my life. I believe he stands on the sideline, allowing me to work out the journey for myself; however, there are times when I feel a slight nudge towards a certain direction.

I have brushed shoulders with many angels walking amongst us. I feel connected, although no words are exchanged. I can't say they have gossamer wings—in fact they look pretty much the same as you and me. They are usually silent but confident in whom they are; their grace speaks for them. One might ask what their work is. Well, it seems to me they have quite a list of duties because they are found in every walk in life, quietly working to make things better.

Often a passing stranger looks directly at me; our eyes meet, perhaps over a counter, across the street, or passing close by, and their soft smiles draw me to them. In my volunteering, I am surrounded by angels who wear uniforms and speak in medical terms; others clean the bathrooms, empty waste bins—duties no less essential. They are cloaked in an aura of compassion, and their care is unreserved. Duties are performed efficiently and effectively, no different than so many others, but angels tenderly touch and nurture the soul too. You know one when you meet one.

Is it an angel who silently fills the coffee pot when the last cup is taken previously, who carries your bags of groceries to the car when your arms are full, or touches your heart with empathy and you are moved to selfless action? Who placed the thought to call me when I needed to hear that particular voice? If I put my keys down and hunt for frantic minutes, then find them in a place I had already checked, did Michael put them there? Anonymous good deeds surround us. There are a lot of clues. Who cannot be influenced to want to do better? I hear angels get their reward in heaven; there is no expectation from us. The Bible reports an angel brought Mary the news she would have a child of God, and in due course an angel announced the birth of that child, Jesus Christ. Christians have celebrated his birth for over two thousand years. Glorious music has been composed that takes the listener to a heavenly peace, and we sing words that prod us to excel. Pictures of glorious beings in sublime repose are often portrayed on cards we exchange to send wishes of joy, peace and love. I am certain angels are by our side, or one step in front, one behind, and remain so. Disasters and heart wrenching physical and emotional pain can sweep us away; so quickly, our faith is tested and sometimes cannot hold up. I've been there. It took a long time to open my heart and trust again. It started with those soft smiles from strangers passing by. Eventually, I could smile back. My body permitted pain to leave, and I stepped onto a new path. I stumbled often but those silently walking with me cheered me on until I eventually reached a resting place. I believe I am a physically and emotionally strong person but that journey was a struggle I could not have handled alone. It took a while to recognize the aloneness was my own allusion; when I opened my mind, the help I needed came to me quietly. No words are required when you feel a gentle hand on your shoulder that feeds energy and encouragement into your heart.

No matter what comes my way, I have hope because I believe in angels. Michael and a team are walking with me. We fall out of step from time to time, but no matter, we are all going in the same direction, and I'm so very glad to have them along!

I HAVEN'T A CLUE

I begin a lot of sentences with *why*? I'm irritating, I know, but I wish *I haven't a clue* wasn't the recurring response back to me. Family and friends are immune to my questioning and tune me out. I've tested it. I once announced, "I'm having a heart attack," in a puny voice that trembled appropriately. My Nan and Grandpa turned off their hearing aids.

Many of the questions asked of me may as well be in a foreign language. Watching a foot tap impatiently garrottes my attempt at an actual answer, and *I don't know* surfaces as a reflex, and *why?* still hangs around. If the questioner's face shows superiority but is hesitant, I interpret it to mean they don't know the answer either, so I just make one up and hope to get away with it. If I were asked what bus goes along Kensington High Street, I could reply with confidence, *oh that would be a number thirty.* Or, and this is asked frequently, how do I live without eating meat? *Very well and happily, thank you very much!* But then I have a tendency to lecture, and use adjectives to describe meat eaters that includes *savages.* Further conversation usually ends there.

I haven't a clue—particularly with a dramatic shake of the head, sounds so much more—well, tenacious, perhaps baffling the questioner enough to prevent further inquiry. I like that! I'm going to practice in front of the mirror. *Well, what do you think about this or that, eh? Huh? Oh, I haven't a clue!* How much more intelligent

I sound. Hey, you—what are the seven spiritual laws of success? *I haven't a clue* is not only a satisfactory answer to that question; it's the truth, of course. *What do you know about the core of the Earth?* requires a lot of thought. If I were given enough time, I fantasize I could explain *the inner core of the Earth, as detected by seismology, is a solid sphere about 1,216 km (760 mi) in radius, or about 70% that of the Moon. It is believed to be an iron–nickel alloy, and may have a temperature similar to the Sun's surface, approximately 5778 K (5505 °C).* Wishful thinking, needless to say, but how that would make their eyes glaze over—I dreamed once that I actually gave such an answer. I woke up feeling like a whiz kid. Regretfully, it didn't last beyond me getting out of bed.

NORTON SIMON ART MUSEUM

Walking around the galleries of an art museum is a special treat for me. I often travel the 605 and 210 freeways to the Norton Simon in Pasadena. I like its size—not as large and busy as the Los Angeles County Museum of Art, and the patrons who meander along with me are patient and polite if one needs to stay a while with a particular piece of artwork. The museum was renovated years ago, and now includes small rooms off main galleries. I like the design because one can spend time in an intimate space that is virtually silent. It allows a solitary experience—just you and the art. The silence offers one the luxury of study, a close up that exposes brush strokes, texture and the depth of the palette used. I feel the intensity of the powerful life-size Rodin figures that are set up on the grassy knolls along the walkway to the entrance; their strength, their mass, contrast with the delights of the light and colours of the Impressionists' work that line the walls of the large open space of the main gallery. A print of Cézanne's *Tulips in a Vase* is the current commissionaire's welcome to visitors entering the glass doors of the entrance.

In the first gallery, just to the right, is a small room with walls lined in red silk. Displayed on the right hand wall, surrounded by small pastoral scenes, is one of my favourite paintings. It is not one that catches the eye easily as the colours are subtle, restful, but it calls to me. It is Jean-Desire-Gustave Courbet's seascape *Marine,* painted in 1865-66. A little over 19" x 24", the picture is composed of bands of pale pinks and yellows, and hinges on the abstract. No boat or other typical ocean element is included. The sandy shore is covered in blue and grey tide pools that reflect a blustery autumn sky. No figure explores these craters, perhaps filled with tiny creatures trapped for a limited time by an ebbed tide. Courbet used a palette knife to agitate the surface paint, exposing the lighter shades below. There are no harsh lines, just a blending of colour that draws me in towards the last remnants of a rosy sunset. The desolation brings a chill to my skin, yet I stay to absorb more.

Further on towards the end of the main gallery are several other works by Courbet. They are so varied in subject as well as technique, one questions if they are by the same artist. His gentle landscapes with waterfalls and fauna can be compared to a Gainsborough, but his boats resting on sandy shores or navigating vicious rocks are unquestionably his own. His portraits express lively energy through bold colour, and light in a focused eye holds the viewer for an extra moment.

Two pieces of sculpture have captured me: Degas' *Little Dancer Aged Fourteen* is a 38" high wax figure of a girl dressed in a real bodice of silk and a gauze tutu, wrinkled tights and ballet slippers. She even wears a satin ribbon through her wig of real hair. The figure is completely covered with a fine layer of wax to unify the image while revealing the texture of each piece of fabric. The late nineteenth century public expressed mixed reaction to this arresting figure but my own has always been utter delight.

The other piece I make sure I spend time with is Marino Marini's bronze *Horseman*. When I look upon this 40" high image, I cannot help but smile. The plump Horseman is firmly seated on the ample rump of a horse that calmly gazes down over its left leg—at what, one can only imagine. The rider appears exuberant; his head is tilted upwards towards the sky—his hands rest gently onto the animal's back. To me, this sculpture represents wonder about life and is a celebration of just that. The simplistic style ensures nothing interferes with the peaceful, blissful energy I feel each time I stand in front of it.

The lovely Tranquil Garden, complete with a large pond where dragon flies hover and specimen trees blend to a restful panorama, is a respite for aching feet and an overworked eye. A cup of coffee restores energy so one can continue the stroll through a wonderland. Conversations go on around me but I am oblivious because my concentration is on the remarkable pieces that remain in my mind's eye, and those that are ahead of me. Happily, if my energy level doesn't recoup, I know I can still return again. And again.

SANCTUARY

I needed to buy a new armchair. Coming to the decision was not so difficult. The raspberry pink velvet chair in my bedroom has faded badly. I thought it beautiful when new, but it's next to the sliding doors leading to the garden and gets a direct hit down the right side from the afternoon sunlight. I like this chair. It has a wide seat so that a cushion can be squeezed either side of me whenever I snuggle down in it to read a book or just to stare into space. It is that type of chair—one you can just lose yourself in. I've had it for years—twenty, at least. It has a history: this is where I nursed my babies, where I discovered the length of their eye lashes, the gentle arch of their brows. When they metamorphosed from small helpless bundles to chubby adventurous toddlers, they climbed up into its lap with looks of triumph. There were no complaints when clothes were dumped all over it because I was too lazy to fold and put them away. It embraced me when the first clump of my hair fell onto the book I was reading, and held me tight when the tears fell. When I was feeling weak and nauseated, it was like sitting in a friend's arms—you know, hugged, supported until I grew stronger. It has been a good chair—a partner, actually.

I scouted a few department stores, and sat in woven rattans, wooden rockers, and upholstered high backed designs, but somehow, none quite fitted me. I tried—really. I placed my arms on their straight arms, let my hands relax in my lap, and jiggled my seat to fit into the contour of their seats but I didn't get that sense of cosiness

27

I was looking for. I explored designer boutiques where there was an abundance of very opulent overstuffed chairs and a selection of beautiful fabrics; so many, I was rendered incapable to choose. I must confess it was fun to pretend I could afford even a couple of the raw silks or brocades, and enjoyed the assistant's help in directing me towards contrasts and trims. I was at the point of almost giving in because the persuasion was skilful if subtle. I actually could see the chair in my room—although it was too large and I would need to compress every inch of me to get passed to the armoire, but it certainly looked good in its rich golden silk cover and braided trim. Very good indeed. Fortunately, I came to my senses before signing a contract that would have led to a lot of explaining to my husband.

One afternoon, I wandered into my bedroom and, without thinking, sat in the seat that had the contour of my bottom—the imprint of my back—and I fitted in perfectly. The new chairs I'd sat in had held an impression of me, but only for a fleeting moment; not permanent like this old friend. I curled up, and leaned my head back; my fingers absently rubbed the rough patches along the arms. The garden was growing quiet in the fading light. Starlings and house sparrows gathered a last meal before settling in for the night. The big marmalade cat from next door gliding along the wall, his head down and tail up in a soft curl, showed little interest in the adjacent activity. He was on his way to his own feast lovingly dished out by his elderly owner, Mrs. Potter. I settled in the comfort of the faded velvet. It wasn't long before I found myself fighting my eyelids to stay open, but I nodded off and awoke to cosseting darkness. I got up and switched on the lamp. There was no more garden to look out on but a reflection of me and my friend, looking peaceful together in a room that is cosy and complete. I traced the faint splotches where I'd tried to sponge off ink where my daughter had practiced her letters. It was impossible for her to keep the pen from overlapping the paper. That was when she was five—fifteen years ago. I can tell you exactly when and how that soft stain on the seat cushion came about and the culprit was a small blond haired boy. And those furrows in the fabric are a body-print of me. Grubby and unkempt, I realized the chair had become a chronicle of family events—and must remain. A friend, a true friend, isn't discarded just because it has been around for a while and has a worn skin. I reproached myself for not taking more care of this shabby, misshapen *precious* bulk and determined that would change.

Now gratitude abounds as I sit inside those peaceful arms, listen to the rain, hug a new grandchild or read a book. This chair and I have a stronger than ever connection. How could I ever have considered it being replaced? It is my haven—it is where I belong. The velvet fabric smells fresh these days, and the fading seems less noticeable after a professional cleaning that did not erase any of those precious testimonials of family history. Our treasured custodian now gets plenty of tender care, and resides in a shaded place, away from the glaring sunlight. I believe she is happy.

WAR AND PEACE

I'm in one of those love-hate relationships—you know, where one moment a mere thought of an individual can soften one's countenance, the next, a painful wince takes over. These two extremes vacillate throughout the day because an audacious Mimus Polyglottos stole my affection a few days ago. I am captivated. My "infatuation" is greyish, ten inches tall, and displays bold white bars on narrow shoulders. Mockingbirds are well named. Not only does my small guest have his own repertoire, but interlaces his unique songs with phrases stolen from other feathered aves. He emits the extraordinary impersonations while atop a telephone pole, and stirs my heart.

As dawn hovers, he sets himself up on his established roost, and begins a compilation of elaborate sounds that call to the awakening day. Later, while I work in my garden, I am happily lulled by the melodic sweetness of his voice that is a complement to the abundance of colour and texture in the space surrounding me. Though unimpressive in stature, his beguiling sounds carry wide across his staked territory. He is not perturbed by occasional male challenges; standing aloft the tall pole, he is confident…in control, for he knows a coquettish female will eventually join him in a lively duet.

Clippings on the compost heap and tools put away, I lay in a hammock in harmony with my surroundings. My book unopened, I am lulled into semi consciousness by the serenade that is a backdrop to my content. Suddenly, a thrice-repeated blast erupts. A sharp *tchack* attacks my pleasure, and is rapidly fired several times more. The large dozing black tom that has made my garden his own terrain, dives in the shrubbery and cowers. The sound is piercing—cutting the peace like a frenzied machete. Those tiny stirrups in my ears go mad, threatening to straighten the coiled cochlea. My wailing, "I hate you!" has no influence on this pint-sized tyke. With beak open wide, he discharges an unequivocal whistle that would challenge any cowboy. Still at it, he takes off from his lofty perch, flapping his wings three or four times before coasting to the wall close by. All becomes silent. He elegantly struts the rocky plinth, toes turned out like a Nijinsky reincarnated; then, breaking into a run, he increases speed like a 747 taking off to a distant vista. His song is exuberant as he travels—the master of his instrument.

The tom, with a hesitant glance, comes out from his refuge and stretches rapturously in a shaft of sunlight. I feel my own tranquillity returning. We make a captive audience, the tom and I. We could, of course, escape the daily escapade; however, like drug addicts, our obsession can only be mitigated by another fix. We relax, assured our gifted entertainer will return for his next performance. We have about thirty minutes. I check my watch, and open my book.

WHAT IS ART?

A French play called ART, by Yasmina Reza, centres around a very large canvas depicting obscure blotches. The young man who made the expensive purchase is dismayed when the artwork receives disparaging comments from his friends. The actors square off in their opinions of the canvas, and the picture quickly becomes an excuse to personally attack one another. The painting is prominently displayed on stage throughout the play, thus allowing the audience to question the opinions expressed via a script and to ask themselves, is it art? Viewing the work in such a way is using art to communicate feeling…a method used occasionally in psychiatric outreach where the clients are encouraged to draw what they cannot articulate verbally. Perhaps the lines are clumsy, two dimensional or difficult to decipher but no matter; they talk, rarely without eloquence and insightfulness.

What would our world be like without this avenue that not only allows us to express ourselves, but also makes our lives infinitely richer? The word *art* generally conjures up images of paintings but art can be both functional and aesthetically pleasing. There is little around us that does not begin as a design concept. The cup in which we pour our tea, the pastry we eat with our tea, and even the chair in which we sit while we drink our tea, all began as a concept in someone's imagination. Because art is subjective—meaning something different to each of us—can the question, *what is it?* be answered?

Some people are born to make great art and others to appreciate it. However, for all the complexity that surrounds the subject, art consists of only two things: form and content, or shape and subject. By means of movement, lines, colours, sounds or forms, art is a human activity. Books and study guides often present the basic functions of art as: to adorn, beautify, express, illustrate, mediate, persuade, record, and redefine reality. Picasso's paintings exhibit numerous views of reality all at once. Portraits of his mistresses combine several angles of the single figure or a head study that is both full face and profile; truly an example of aesthetic exploitation of familiarity vs. surprise. The viewer is challenged to work out the confusing composition until rewarded with discovery. Although some fully appreciate what they have been privileged to see, others pass on without awareness.

Whether a spectator in the gallery or a listener to the voice of the world's greatest soprano, it takes commitment and ability to be an audience. Novelist Ann Patchett believes that opera, more than any other art form, has the sheer power and magnitude to pull us into another world. British actor Andy Serkis was quoted as saying he believes art can change the world. Art is considered highly skilled expressions based on certain aesthetic principles and covers many subjects, including conversation, architecture, carving and sculpture, music and cuisine. One can even apply the term to cunning, as defined by the Artful Dodger in Dickens's Scrooge. Our personal adornment or embellishment of clothes, hairstyles, make up, the shape of men's beards and simply the choice of French cuffs are all displays of art, created to project the individual's persona to the world. Clever television and print advertisements persuade one brand is superior to another by using the psychology of association through colourful images. Odes are written to glorify the natural beauty of this planet; sometimes attributing its perfection to a sublime being whose artistry is beyond what a mere mortal could dream. At an exhibit at the Museum of Modern Art in Los Angeles, I watched figures covered in black plastic trash bags roll on the floor. In another room, a man and woman were cutting up pieces of white paper that fell to a black floor covering. Both created compositions that I found fascinating. Children draw images that allow us glimpses into their exquisite fantasy and their purple trees show us a different way to view what is around us.

For all my effort, I cannot define what art is. An adequate definition is too elusive. One can only apply the feeling drawn from whatever is being contemplated at that time to establish an opinion—not a definition. One trip to London involved a very rainy day. Sitting on the top deck of a bus, I overlooked masses of umbrellas being jostled on the crowded pavement below. The shapes, colours and movement created a pattern that pleased my eye. Could that be considered art? It had form and content, and was aesthetically pleasing. What about the misshapen splashes of colour reflected in the wet pavements? Was Sam Francis at work? It could not have been Jason Pollock for he maintained even forms. One question leads to another, and then another. My inability to answer the questions is not only due to my lack of language but also the reluctance to build boundaries around a subject that is so indefinable; it could be only an illusion. Brush strokes confidently applied to a canvas by an elephant or chimpanzee could stand side by side with those of Franz Kline or John Levee. Would I know the difference? Do I care? My pleasure comes from looking, listening, feeling and contemplating all that is around me, and I'm grateful for it.

WHO DO YOU THINK YOU ARE?

Who do I think I am? Well...**Deoxyribonucleic acid** (DNA) is the genetic code for all living life forms and is found in the nucleus of a cell. It is a ladder-shaped molecule, a double helix composed of two parallel strands connected by many "rungs" made up of four nucleotides or amino acid bases, arranged in pairs. The order of the four base pairs is unique to each organism and contains its individual code written as a string of letters—G(guanine), A(adenine), T(thymine) and C(cytosine). Those four letters repeated over and over in a unique mix equal *Me*. I am the end product of such a formula that is influenced by those who make up the branches of my family tree. My hazel eyes come from my mother, my chin from my father. The arthritis in my fingers is thanks to my maternal grandmother, and my height seems to be controlled by a certain gene passed on from Little Granny, her mother. Who I am is also a matter of chance. If Mary Godwin had married my grandfather Richard Dawson all those generations ago, instead of poet Percy Shelley, perhaps I would be writing in the genre of the macabre. Instead, Grandfather Dawson fell for the lively Faith Allen, and my fate was sealed in a completely different direction.

A couple of branches of the family tree reveal my kin as farmers. Perhaps my love of the land and the effort I put in to cultivate my own small plot is the thread that connects me to them. If those humble folk are looking down on me, I would appreciate their guidance as I toil with spade and hoe to plant a drought tolerant landscape to counter the developing brown lifeless site. Blisters like miniature opaque balloons float across my palms, and a couple of unlady-like calluses are testimony to my labour, but I do not complain. My oasis in the midst of suburbia is a peaceful haven that I survey with sweet pleasure.

As a vegetarian, I feel a connection to those far distant ancestors who survived on a meatless diet. According to many respected anthropologists, walking upright was developed in order to reach fruits and nuts ripening above in trees. The sticky pests living amongst the foliage added texture to such fare as well as protein, but what about the taste? Of course, it was a long, long stretch in time before that event, but it makes sense because the mushy over-ripe bounty that fell to the ground and became coated in dirt and insects must have eventually lost appeal. Did our ancestors' yearning for flavour and variety force exploration to find more tempting chow? I can imagine many scenarios when flesh was first tasted. An old carcass rotting in the sun could not have been very appetizing, but a clean one roasting in the sun would have got the saliva running. I cannot relate to those in my past who were daring enough to take a first bite. Those in my present who tuck into a blooded steak or sing raptures over a fillet of sole cannot relate to me either. Perhaps the line I come from remained looking and reaching up. Did fruits and nuts—along with a leaf or two, suit them enough to prevent their further exploration?

Over the years, the question, *who do you think you are?* has been asked of me more than a few times. It was said in such a way as to suggest I'm too big for my shoes—a little above myself. Emphasis on *little*, of course! Why is that so? Physical differences or an opinion that differs from another's must not be suppressed even if it is not easy to accept. As an art student, I stood out amongst my friends who attended a business college. *Who do you think you are?* came up then, but I just fluttered my black kohl-encircled eyes and jingled the fifteen brilliantly coloured bangles imported from India that covered my left arm to the elbow. I do not like that question. It pulls me down, and I resent it. I want questions that evoke answers that push me to a higher level, but I now know my promotion to any level is up to me—*who do you think you are?* is a question only I can answer. Do I draw on the fertile genetic pool from whence I came or am I just this sixty-two inch tall female who fills a certain amount of space? The twists and turns in my journey to this point, and all the decisions I have made thus far, are predicated on awareness and gut feelings that are possibly predisposed by the experience of those from whom I draw my DNA. Could the inner voice I carefully listen to be the unified family chorus of all those who stand in the heavens, watching my every move—perhaps with their own questions: *will she? won't she?* When my mind tells me *this way*, is it that interfering gang up there telling me *that way*? The dilemma can be disconcerting, but those voices are a part of me. If asked now who do I think I am, I say proudly—I'm *Them*!

Poetry

∞

AQUAMAN

See him balanced on thickly applied resin,
Achieving an off-the-lips akin to Mr Richards,
Easily scooping clear of inquisitive playful pod,
Freewheeling while foam-spray lazily calms.

Salt crystals swathe raw bronzed features,
Hair ridiculed and whipped by briny gusts.
A serious image that both occupies, identifies
The courage awaiting the Goliath of the set.

Ocean and horizon fuse without division.
Swells surge then gently retreat to slumber
As perfect rhythm lulls all thought, emotion,
Except that of quiet, patient anticipation.

Eyes crinkle against the piercing glare,
The growing distant roar trounces lethargy
And heart quickens to snap back rapidly.
At-the-ready to skim escalating mighty surge.

The body lifts, stands erect and kicks out.
Board thrusts rider into tube of green opaque.
Then reappears to sashay remaining undulation
Till shallows harness his racing-rocket high.

Spirits blend elements into a single dimension.
Perched fearlessly over mysterious metropolis
The rider achieves desired flawless cloud-break
Then awaits approaching set as his reward.

BROTHER

What is it you want? Your staring eyes
So solemn, such blatant interest.
Yes, this is my home, a single bench
Achingly cold, where I lay to rest.
My muscles are compressed by its imprint.
This thin, worn blanket my only defence.

What can you do to help my desperation?
Can you spare a few coins to abate my thirst?
Or more for a bowl of hot Mission soup?
Dare I hope for a job and a room?
Or is it enough for you to just look
Then walk on with a mind clear of me?

I talk with myself, sometimes shout aloud.
Bile choking the fear in my throat.
I had it together, and then blamelessly fell.
You may think ill of me but I still have pride.
It is still there, struggling deep inside.
So I cannot, must not, give up but hope.
Will help come from you? Can I believe
You will save me, so I can live again?

CYCLE RACE

Feet adorned in bright tight strapping
Fight hard against that invisible wall
Of unyielding airstream pushing back.
Piston-pumping knees build pressure
Muscles bunch, slick with heated sweat.
But excitement intensifies the force.

Rivers of salt run from scalp,
Stinging eyes and stealing the view.
Weary shoulders parallel to the challenge
Force fatigued limbs to boost the pace.
Shortened breath struggles in gulps,
Challenging the effort to pull out front.

No coasting to rest only continual motion.
Head low, resolute to take the curves.
Energy now lagging but cannot concede
Till exhausted silent screams of relief
Divide the others into one at the finish line,
And winner takes the coveted prize.

HUMMING BIRD

Look, it's a shimmering haze
Of green and vermilion.
Alacrity, it darts and swoops,
Then hovers on a blur of wings
That flap at eighty times a blink.
No larger than an ostrich eye,
It makes a dash to purple sage,
To suck deep on tasty wine
Till thirst and hunger fades.
Fuelled on syrupy nectar,
It whizzes away to rest.
Then fifteen minutes later
Returns to feast again
For energy is rapidly spent.

A tuneless chirp of bliss begins
From throat of iridescent tint.
Not a humming as rumoured,
But a buzz sublime and sweet.
I sit very still to gaze upon
A creature supposedly elusive.
Suspended, it checks me out,
Then comes in closer to stare.
I return that gaze with silence,
And know our allure is shared.
Abruptly, the space is emptied,
Our brief union is over.
Without regret I look ahead,
And smile softly and reflect.

INNOCENCE LOST

Young eyes are fixed on the overflow
Of colour and shape in the tormented sky.
Wind contorts golden islands of cloud,
Unanchored, free to go where they will.
Tinkling gleeful laughter rings out
From Child who sees only perfection.

The sun dapples the shoreline vista
With reflective shafts of light.
Breeze blows tunefully, playfully,
Stroking ribbons of yellow tresses.
Splashing feet tangle and collapse,
And Child is flushed with delight.

Waves tenderly caress that dimpled silk,
Forever mindful of their precious charge.
Ocean beads fall from chubby fingers
Dampening the warm sandy ground.
Wondrous Child at one with Nature,
Sees only World of beauty all around.

Suddenly ominous shadows emerge,
And inject Mankind's terrible Legacy
To contaminate innocence and joy.
Laughter is silenced as tears pour out
Now fear and torment are released.
And Purity and Trust is lost to Child,

Love is the combatant to that brutal act.
The strength of such devotion is rallied
And can heal those lacerations of doubt.
Enduring care will restore the Child
So lovingly cherished, never given up,
Rectitude will make certain of that.

MIGRAINE

A deep chasm edged with scarlet.
Pounding agony throughout the night,
Eye sockets scorched with pain;
Medicine come quickly, end this plight.

Rapid ease longingly sought.
But time slowly passes before relief.
Tolerable light now gradually accepted,
Mind opening, able to form a thought.

Beautiful world welcome me back,
To be free again without restriction.
Stop this torture; release is essential
For me to move on to full potential.

PRESSURE FOR PERFECTION

Why can't I just say grass is green?
Why isn't it enough?
Why do I struggle to describe exactly the hue?
Could it be because my ego is involved?
Could I have something to prove?
Could it be that simple? Alas, not simple for me,
For Nature made the grass and chose the perfect colours.
Not one green but others.
Blue, bluish, dark green.
Yellow, yellowish, light green.
I feel a duty to paint accurately with words
To give Her work justice.

Contrasts in light, depth, and colour changes
Reflect from the polished face of every blade
That spreads over dales, filling gaps and fissures.
A living overcoat that both warms and cools the land,
And nurtures life sustained by such a perfect plan.
Restful to the eye is every green,
Restful to the eye of our soul.

My duty proves a challenge,
My mind must work the canvas
Then I can rest.

SALCOMB BAY

Lathered up surf like soapy shaving water
Steals away the cool granules of sand,
And tickles my wriggling puckered toes,
As I dance on a sun-kissed shore.

Tough dune grass gathers nomad grains
While greedily sucking salty moisture
To build soft walls of defiance
To the tune of a whistling squall.

Sandpiper dares the wandering tide
That spreads delicate periphery of bubbles.
Bill ventures deep with rapid speed
To snatch a tasty sliver of crustacean.

Waves whooshing, crashing, retreating,
Spraying damp freckles on my smiling face.
There is oneness in this magical moment,
It is an encompassing energetic embrace.

Oh, Salcomb Bay, so full of bliss
There, on the southern coast of Devon.
I travel far but always return to where
Those years of memories make it heaven.

TAKING A CHANCE

Hand trembling, hesitating yet determined,
Reaching out with rapid, sneaky movement—snatching.
Heart racing, fingers spastic with fear,
While tearing crackling wrapper from the prize.

Smooth luxurious satin, the chocolate melting,
Coating teeth, tongue, holding off swallowing—savouring.
This is ecstasy, this is wealth.
Relishing, lips tightly closed, no clue allowed to escape.
No sharing this delight—with anyone!

Wrappers folded over and over, foil a tiny ball.
Where to put them? This is evidence, no pocket deep enough.
Must find secret cover up.
Eyes darting—not here, not there, but where?

Heavy pressure on shoulder felt, heart bursting panic!
Hand pried open for all to see the tell-tale testimony.
Led off in despondency, shame, every eye turning,
Focusing, judging; I'm shrinking—how to survive?
Door! Go—get through on wobbling sticks.

Released from observation but humiliation lives.
Lesson learned not to be forgotten.
Never take what is not freely given—for all is not mine
Although, I believe it should be!

WE CAN …

How do We make it?
Who will show the way?
Life's lessons learned
Too often lead us astray.

Destructive instruction
Reaps havoc, pain.
Such piercing emotions
Can cause love to wane.

Determination and belief
In We is what it takes.
To revaluate, dedicate,
And continue to debate.

The uplift of our joy
Cannot be repressed.
You see, You and Me,
The *We*—are the best.

ANNIVERSARY

It is We, you and me—years later.
Much time for learning and accepting
As resistance crumbles to dust, and fades.

It is We—now in harmony.
Liberated spirits stretching and exploring
Till peace cradled our souls, and we rest.

It is We—in agreement.
Single-minded, believing in the unknown
That is unconditionally certain, amazingly so.

It is We—much time has passed.
Now We abide in a continuum of moments
Of joy, commitment, and a love that will last.

And now We are no longer afraid.
Lovingly sheltered in a safe warm embrace
We confidently celebrate all that We are.

WINTER AHEAD

There is a nip in the thinning air,
Enough to shrink and blue the skin.
Shadows reach farther now
And douse the weakening sun.
Russet leaves rustle animated
And drift to blanket a dozing land.

Hurry life, eat while you may.
Fatten yourself as the larder empties.
Sap falls to roots for safety
Controlled by elements without mercy.
Wild storms flex their mighty power,
Darkening clouds scream and spin.

Feathered fliers use map of stars
By moonlight behind an opaque veil.
Gluttonous frenzy is over now,
Replaced by impatient longing
To travel afar with your kind,
To that warmer land called home.

Builders gather your materials,
Apply your inherent survival plans.
Hasten to fill those secret pantries,
Weave soft webs and yellow grasses
To insulate against the coming force.
Then you can then sleep safe and warm.

Burrowers dig with sharpened claws,
Deep into the cold dark earth.
Hollow out fissures and crannies,
And ferret for luscious grubs and roots

To stock a winter bounteous hoard.
For your survival will depend on it.

Now it is time to prepare for slumber.
The land must slow and rest awhile.
Impotent sun pretends it strength
While night nibbles at shortening days.
Lavender haze softens the horizon,
And all is calm under Nature's gaze.

Short Stories

∞

ANOTHER CHANCE

Dust particles played chase in the shafts of sunlight breaking through two tall windows. A tufted-eared marmalade cat lounged on one of the windowsills, eyes half closed as it watched a green budgerigar swinging on a perch in an elaborate white pagoda. Freshly plumped cushions covered in the same material as the colourful curtains stood at attention on the couch. The television was a monotone invasion, and entertained no one. A tinkling of a china cup against a saucer announced the occupant of this cosy, immaculate apartment. She was a large woman, wearing an overall emblazoned with flowers in all colours. The pelmet of skirt below was black; so too were the stockings covering thick, defiant legs. A pair of chequered brown slippers with a pompom atop each encased her wide feet. "Pretty boy!" she called to the bird, her voice frail, contrasting to her solid physical presence. She placed the cup of tea on a small table, and sat down in the armchair positioned purposely in the weak winter sunlight. After a while, warmth penetrated her tired bones; her body relaxed and melted into the comfort. She leaned her head back, at ease. Time passed slowly, the ticking clock competed with the voices on the television; companions for a lonely seventy-five year old widow.

Afternoon shadows lengthened across the room. The cat rose and stretched like pulled taffy; yawing, it exposed its lethal weapons. The woman stirred too; her inward clock had announced the routine nap was over. Slowly, she got up out of the chair, and took the teacup into the kitchenette. Five o'clock. Another day almost over; they stacked one upon the other, just like the dishes in the cabinet on the wall in front of her: neat, uniform, and neutral in colour. The doorbell interrupted her melancholy. Who could it possibly be at this hour? She hesitantly made her way to the front door, and called out, "Who's there?" She opened the door a couple of inches and peered out with dull eyes through rimless glasses. A smiling blond woman was standing on the step.

"Hello, Mrs. Walker, my name is Jackie Singleton. I'm a volunteer with the local support group for the elderly. Your name and address was given to me by your doctor's office because you are in my area. Can I come in for a minute? I know it's a little late, but it's the first chance I've had all day and I want to introduce you to our program."

"Yes, it is late. I wasn't expecting company."

"I'll only take a moment," Jackie answered, stepping through the door.

Ignoring Florence's frosty stare, Jackie sat in a comfortable armchair. She took out several notes from a briefcase and proceeded to explain the program she helped run. "Mrs. Walker...or can I call you Florence? It is friendlier, don't you think?"

"I suppose."

"Thank you...and please call me Jackie." She handed Florence a brochure. "This will help explain the program details. Twice a week, Mondays and Wednesdays, we can pick you up and take you to the Senior Centre. We have all kinds of activities, and you can get to know our other seniors. It'll be a fun time, and will get you out in the community. I'll leave this brochure so you can read all about it."

"I have no interest, really." Florence's face was set.

Jackie's voice softened. "Won't you give it a chance? You'll make friends and have lunch there. It really is a most pleasant place. We can pick you up on Monday, around ten. We have to pick others up on the way so you will need to be ready." Jackie gathered up the papers, extending a hand as she stood up. Florence's hand felt lifeless and Jackie gave it a gentle squeeze. "I'll let myself out, Florence. I really hope you decide to join us on Monday. We'll stop by, just in case."

She opened the office door and entered a bleak room furnished with leftovers gathered from who-knows-where. The icy wind had torched Jackie's nose. Fine droplets formed a velvet sheen across the shoulders of her coat. She sat at her desk and shivered as the electric fire strained to warm the small area. She took out Florence's file from her briefcase. The notes were few and validated the doctor's concern for yet another isolated member of society. Jackie was well aware of the troubling situation in the community. Family structure had changed drastically over the years for many reasons; mostly financial pressures or coping with life challenges in general. A safe place for a frail member within the household, particularly the elderly, was hardly the tradition any more. Like so many others, Florence had silently acquiesced to her confined life, but Jackie determined she would change that and reawaken Florence's spirit.

Monday appeared bright, but frigid. The tree limbs looked black against the grey rain-heavy sky; birds huddling in the leafless branches had fluffed out their feathers to try to keep warm. The small white van parked in front of Florence's home was on time. Jackie was delighted to see Florence was wearing her coat when she answered the door. Earlier, Florence had sat on the edge of her bed and considered the opportunity to experience something different. She felt both excitement and anxiety after deciding to accept. She chose to wear a blouse worn only once before, the colour bringing out the blue of her eyes. It lessened the pallor of her face too, but not its unyielding demeanour. She was afraid to soften, to feel. It cost too much. Jackie was aware of Florence's apprehension as she helped her into the van. They picked up three other passengers—each one greeting Florence with a cheery hello.

The Centre was in a new red brick building tucked onto the end of a grand gothic church; the disparity between the traditional structure and the modern bungalow with lots of glass was striking and they seemed at odds with each other. Cheery in a yellow sweater, a tall, bespectacled man was waiting to greet them. His young companion, her long chestnut curls dancing in the wind, helped him steer the flock into the warmth. She took Florence's arm as Florence slowly, insecurely, stepped along the path. "Thank you, dear." The girl smiled. "You're welcome."

It took some time to get everyone settled. Florence sat on a hard chair, refusing to participate in any craft or the sing-a-long. She clutched her handbag to her chest, and looked straight ahead. Jackie allowed her to be, and was encouraged when Florence guardedly accepted a cup of tea. The tea seemed to break the ice, for Florence allowed herself a quick glance around the large room with about twenty people milling about. Enthusiastic players lined up in front of a dartboard, noisily egged each other on. In a comfortable seating area, a table had a tea urn and tins of biscuits laid out. A bearded man and a couple of women relaxing in armchairs had helped themselves. It was then Florence saw the young woman who had greeted her when she arrived at the Centre. Florence watched for a while; there was something about the girl that touched her. Her laughter was childlike, innocent, and her open smile seemed to flow from deep within. Florence turned to the woman seated next to her who was working with deft fingers to create a table mat; her hands were so thoroughly trained, concentration was unnecessary.

"That young girl over there, who is she?"

"Oh, that's Jenny. She earns pocket money by doing odd jobs here each week. She lives at the orphanage, although she's not a kid anymore."

"What's wrong with her?"

"She's a retard...you know, brain damaged. Can't speak properly. She's a sweet girl though, with the loveliest smile" Her manner was matter-of-fact.

When lunch was wheeled into the dining area, Jenny went up to Florence and asked if she was ready to take off her coat. Florence had purposely kept it on as her badge of defiance, wanting everyone to know she had no intention of staying; however, to her own surprise, she found it difficult to hold back from the girl and slipped the coat from her shoulders, emerging as if from a cocoon in the blue blouse with a cameo brooch at her throat. Always observant, Jackie was encouraged by the attention Florence had given to her appearance.

With less apprehension, Florence went to the Centre again on Wednesday, and again watched Jenny. She thought the girl looked pale, drawn for one so young, and she felt concern. Perhaps the youngster was overworked, trying to be at every one's beck and call? Florence thought of her own children; she had four—four strangers now, each living successful lives, with no time for her any longer. Even her grandchildren treated her with cool indifference because they hardly knew her.

"Time to go, Florence." Florence was surprised to see Jackie holding her coat. Where had the day gone?

She turned the key in the lock and stepped into a room that seemed sterile, devoid of life. Even the cat curling around her ankles in welcome had no effect. Automatically, she turned on the television, needing to fill the noisy quiet. The apartment had always been her safe haven, so much a part of her, yet it now seemed overbearing, pressing in. She needed to feel someone close, to not feel so completely alone. Without warning, heavy tears broke from her eyes. She unsteadily sank into the armchair and covered her face.

Jenny walked quickly. She wore a special boot that was hidden by her slacks. It had taken a lot of practice to not show a limp, and she was proud of her accomplishment. The wind was strong, holding her long hair behind her like a horse's mane, wild and free. She pushed her gloved hands deep inside her coat pockets and shivered. A gust of freezing air grabbed at her briefly before letting go with a shove, destabilizing her balance and composure. Florence opened the front door and stared in disbelief. A white, pinched face stared back, eyes wide, uncertain.

"Jenny! What a lovely surprise."

Jenny's mouth turned up in a grin of relief, teeth white against her chapped lips. She held out a small, crumpled envelope.

"Your brooch."

"Goodness, I wondered what had happened to it." She grasped Jenny's arm and gently led her into the warm apartment. "That brooch is very important to me. I would be very sad if I didn't get it back. How did you know it was mine?"

"Jackie told me to bring it to you. She gave me your address and told me how to get here." Her voice was out of tune, some words were incomplete and rushed, as if needing to get out before forgotten. She made for the cat. She pressed her nose against the warm soft fur; delighted her attention was accepted.

"You have come a long way. Take your coat off for a few moments and sit by the fire. You must be frozen." Jenny had difficulty coping with the buttons on the coat. Florence did not offer to help but went into the kitchenette. "I'll make you a hot drink."

"I did it, Flo', I took my coat off." The girl called.

"I knew you could."

Florence brought in a steaming cup, the smell of chocolate was strong. She smiled as Jenny slurped noisily from the cup. She noticed Jenny's sweater and slacks were worn, likely hand-me-downs. A seam of the sweater was held together by large unmatched stitches. Perhaps they were Jenny's own repair work. "How did you get involved with the Senior Centre?"

"I'm grown up now. I had to get a job. Not in a shop or anything, that would be too hard for me. Jackie works with adoptions at the orphanage and one day she asked if I'd like to help her at the Centre. She needed someone to make tea and meet the visitors—things like that I can do well. I make good tea."

"That's true. You make excellent tea! I don't know what they'd do without you! Are you in a hurry? Can you stay a while?" Florence's voice was soft but prepared for rejection. "I can make us something to eat."

"If I'm late, they'll worry. I'll come again," she said cheerfully. She placed the empty cup on the table and reached for her coat.

Florence watched from the window as the girl hurried along the street, her figure bent against the wind. Suddenly she stopped, turned and waved—involving every part of her small body in the effort; then she was gone.

A fresh tablecloth covered the small table in front of the fire; two chairs were placed across from each other. A sponge cake and crustless sandwiches invited sampling. Almost one o'clock. Jenny should be arriving any minute. Florence gently lifted the cat from her lap and peered through the window. Four months had passed since she first saw Jenny at the Centre. Four months of slow thawing. She had tried to hold back at the beginning, yet found herself looking forward to Mondays and Wednesdays, if only to see the girl. It had been a long time since she had looked forward to anything. She knew Jenny, too, looked forward to seeing her. As soon as the van drew up, she ran out to escort Florence, holding tightly onto her arm. The rhythm of the ticking clock became intrusive. It was now two-thirty, and still no Jenny. What could have happened? Maybe she missed the bus—perhaps she had forgotten? Florence's fingers absently worried a couple of crumbs on the cloth. By now the heat of the fire had dwindled. The cake's icing had sweated and the sandwiches were drying out. She had taken pleasure in preparing the things she thought Jenny would like. She cleared the table as her anxiety increased.

The knocking was urgent. Florence hurried to open the door, and peered into Jenny's anxious eyes. "I missed the bus and had to walk. It was a very long way." Her voice was reproachful. Florence took her hand and drew her inside.

"I've been so worried." Her voice broke with relief.

"I got you a present." Jenny said smugly. "Jackie told me it's your birthday tomorrow." She held out a wrinkled package.

Florence felt childlike pleasure as she removed the white tissue paper and exposed pink satin slippers. "Oh, Jenny, they're so pretty."

"Those brown slippers belong to a grandpa. You're not a grandpa, Florence."

"You're quite right. They are ugly old things." She quickly put the new slippers on and held out her feet, smiling broadly. "These are beautiful, the very best slippers I've ever had."

She reset the table while Jenny took off her coat and sought out the cat. The emptiness they had both known for so long had begun to fill.

Over the next few weeks, the two learned to trust, and love was given freely one to the other until they became inseparable. Jackie helped Jenny move into Florence's spare room. It didn't take long. Jenny had few possessions to place around the small room with pink striped wallpaper. It was the first room of her own, and more than a few tears of joy were shed. One evening, Jenny sat on the arm of Florence's chair. "Flo', I want to tell you about why I don't want to go to see anyone at the orphanage any more. I don't always understand things, and because of the way I talk, they get mad with me. They call me stupid, and that hurts my feelings. I don't have to go there now I live with you, do I Flo'?"

"You don't have to do anything you don't want to ever again." Florence felt anger rising. How blind some people can be. Didn't they realise how much Jenny had overcome? "You are smart and very special. They don't know what they are talking about. You forget them, Jenny. You will never have to see or talk with them again." She reached out and took the girl's hand. "I've hurt, too. My husband got ill but I didn't know how bad he was. The doctor didn't know either. When he died, my children thought I hadn't cared."

"You mean your children got mad with you like those at the orphanage got mad with me?"

"Yes, very mad. I don't hear from them very much anymore." She became quiet, remembering: she and her husband were happily married for many years. She smiled wistfully. "My husband was from a seaside town, and loved sailing. When our children learned to sail, he was so proud of them. We had glorious holidays; we barbecued on the beach...rode our bikes. The children grew like beanstalks until they towered over me, just like their father." She looked far away. "I

64

used to love to swim, and that's how my husband and I met. I was swimming in a lake and he went by in his dinghy, and kept splashing me until I gave up and got on board. He was full of fun." She laughed. "He gave me that brooch you found. I saw it in a jeweller's window and the next thing I knew, he'd bought it for me. He was like that. I suppose it's hard for you to think of me as young and a swimmer. I was good at it, and won quite a few trophies. I taught my children." She paused and looked at Jenny. "Would you like to learn? I could teach you. I'm not a youngster but still know how." She sighed quietly. "It all seems so long ago."

"Will your children be my family now?"

"I would like that but one by one they moved away. I miss them a lot. Their hearts were broken when they lost their father...mine was broken too."

"Flo', I'll be your family now, and then your heart will get mended."

"My heart is already mending now you are here." She smiled. "My dear Jenny."

"Where are your children? What are their names, Flo'?"

"My son Stephen lives only a few miles from here. He is named for his father. Richard is in London, and Lisa is in Surrey. Jane lives in another country called Australia."

"Do you know how to get to them?"

"I get a letter each Christmas from Jane. From time to time the others send a note or phone, and mention possibly visiting me here, but then something usually happens and they don't make it. They send me money every month so I have everything I need, but I'd so like a visit instead, especially from my grandchildren. They're grown up now, but Stephen's daughter Anne is still a teenager like you." Florence's voice strained with emotion. "I've missed my family, Jenny. I've been very lonely."

"We are alike, Flo'." She looked closely at Florence. "You have me now, and I have you, so we won't be lonely anymore. I'll be your new granddaughter. I remembered your birthday, didn't I?" She moved to Florence's lap, and put her head on her shoulder "I had friends at school and wasn't so lonely then, but I couldn't keep up with the lessons. I did try. I knew some of the answers but the words got mixed up. I was put in special classes but they were still too hard for me. Some kids called me a retard and that made me cry. They said my mother and father didn't want me because I was ugly and stupid."

Florence stroked Jenny's curls. "What do those silly kids know? I can assure you, my dear; they have their own pain and hide it by hurting others."

"That's weird. I don't understand, Flo'."

"It is complicated, but I promise what they said means nothing. Just silly sounds that make no sense so release them from you mind. You won't be seeing them again."

"I'm glad." She kissed Florence's cheek. "You're clever, Flo'."

"I'm clever all right, and know for certain your mother and father loved you with all their hearts. It must have been so very painful for them to give you up. Jackie said they were very young and couldn't keep you for several reasons but I am sure they tried really hard. Sometimes things don't work out as we would like. What they decided must have been for the very best reasons. You will always be a part of them and, of course, they are a part of you. They would be so proud to see what a beautiful young woman you are." She smiled.

"You think I'm beautiful, Flo'? When ladies and men came to see the kids, they never wanted to see me. Then I got older so I knew I wouldn't get adopted, ever."

"If I'd known you then, I'd have adopted you." Florence hugged Jenny to her. "Don't be sad any longer. We have each other now, and yes, you will be my new granddaughter." Jenny pressed herself against Florence—her small body fitted perfectly in Florence's arms.

"Shall I call you Grandmother?"

"If you like. Flo's all right though."

"I think I'll choose…" She put her finger to her lip and giggled with delight. "Umm—Grandmother!"

"That's settled then!"

There was no pity as each told their story; the words rushed out, cleansing. The past was moving away, and they were starting anew. Jenny settled herself in front of the fire, with the cat on her lap. Florence went into the kitchenette to start dinner.

"Grandmother, I can give you the money I earn at the Centre?"

"My sweet girl, I've got more than enough of my own. The money you work for is yours. In fact, we should go shopping, have some fun. Let's go tomorrow." She started to set the table. "You can buy something you really like. Now, wash up; dinner is almost ready."

It took a while for Jenny and Florence to adjust to living together, but their commitment to each other quickly melted any apprehension. Jenny began speech therapy, and her new grandmother began knitting again. Through Jenny's urging, Florence sent a modest card to her son, Stephen. It said simply, *miss you.* To their surprise—delight, he telephoned. Jenny answered. "Grandmother, come quickly."

Bluebells had transformed the woods behind the Centre. Florence stepped forward as the van drove up. "Fresh coffee inside. Glad you could make it today, Tom. You are looking much better. Jenny, give Mrs. Jason a hand with her bag, will you, dear?" She took delight in playing the role of mother hen. A warm smile and encouraging words came easily. She had rediscovered herself through the joy of having Jenny in her life. No one knew exactly why, but the Centre had also gone through its own transformation. It was as if the members had experienced a unifying jolt of kinship, for they became even more close-knit and watchful of each other. Several young people from an assisted living facility were now regulars. A few disabled veterans had joined too. Florence put her arm around Jenny's shoulders as they hurriedly made their way out of the building. It was spring, the time of anticipation and hope, and Stephen and his family was due at 4 o'clock.

BEST OF FRIENDS

No matter how warm it got at night during that summer, my wife and I fastened every window in the house tight! It was the only way to shut out the threats showered on us by our once friendly now alienated neighbours. You see, our dog Bess had suddenly become a barker! She barked not only at normal things dogs bark at, you know, cats, strangers and the like; but she barked at, well—everything. My unsuccessful attempts to stop her made me suspicion she didn't care for me as much as I thought. Surely, she wouldn't put me through so much sleep deprivation, tongue lashings by ex-friends, and worse— threats from my wife that I would soon be residing in other premises. The noise would start just as the lights were turned out; the signal to begin her overture.

One night she really got carried away, and our neighbours created an upsurge of angry threats questioning my heritage. The incessant fussing went on all night. When dawn broke, there was no energy left to invest in anything but sleep. I stole a glance through the window and saw Bess pacing. Too weary to hassle with her, I got back into bed beside my fuming wife, and consciousness faded.

I awoke with a thick head and a rotten mouth, but also to sweet silence. Hesitantly, I got up and peered out the window. Bess was asleep. I whistled tunelessly as I showered. The water was hot and invigorating. My body relaxed, and I began to plan a visit to my irate neighbours to apologize dutifully, if not totally sincerely. I turned the water off and held my breath. Peace! The smell of coffee wafted up from the kitchen as my wife prepared breakfast before leaving to spend the day with her sister. I wrapped a towel around my waist and went to join her just as the barking started up again. I felt real hate as I raced to the garden. Bess was in front of the door of the shed—nose down, teeth bared, a line of hair standing straight up along her back. Each bark consumed her, shaking her balance.

"What's gotten into you?" I slapped her rump sharply.

She pushed in front, determined. I pulled open the door a few inches and peered into the gloom. There was movement in the far corner and I spread a leg across the entrance to hold back my now lunatic dog who was ready to charge. There was a whimper from within, so soft, it was a miracle I heard it over the racket. I slammed the door shut and grabbed Bess. It took all my strength to get her over to the chain stake, and I returned to the shed with mounting curiosity. With the door open all the way, light exposed the jumble of forgotten things. Cobwebs clung to my face as I made my way inside. I pulled back a deck chair with fabric frayed and faded. Whatever lay behind shrank into itself and I felt the fear in both of us. There was a sudden flash of brown as something ran passed me, startling me so that I landed on top of an old skateboard discarded long ago. The towel around my waist fell unnoticed.

"If you don't let Bess off that chain, she'll do herself in." Joe, my know-it-all twenty year old son stood with hands on hips; his normally dull features wore a puzzled expression. It took a moment before he zeroed in to my nakedness and his eyebrows shot up. "What's with you, Dad?"

My exasperation overtook any modesty. "Try to quiet Bess down. Can't you see I've trouble here—and stop staring?" My eyes scouted the garden and came to rest on a mud splattered, shivering shadow of what appeared to be a retriever trying to make itself invisible under a bush. I slowly walked up to it and placed my hand on his head. His eyes rolled back with fear. "It's all right, boy." Talking continuously, I carefully felt along the length of his back and was relieved there were no injuries. Eventually I felt him relax. I was grateful; my legs were numb from bending. I called to Joe to put Bess in the garage and, with great care, picked up the quivering bundle. I sat down on a garden chair, and balanced the scrawny body across my legs, my nudity long forgotten. "There's a good old boy. I bet you're hungry and thirsty. Hey, Joe! Bring me some water…and a piece of whatever Mum put out for dinner."

I held the water under the dog's nose for a long time and continued to talk softly. Eventually, his tongue, dry and white, lapped up the cool liquid. "Try to get a little of this down you too, lad." He must have been ravenous, but it took a supreme effort for him to swallow the smallest piece of chicken. "Good boy." His eyes closed. I left him comfortable on the chair.

"Wait 'til Mum learns about the chicken. What's going on?" Joe demanded.

"I wish I knew. There's no collar; he could have come from anywhere. He jumped the fence and hid in the shed."

"Looks like he's been through it."

"Yes, I bet he has a story to tell, poor lad. He can stay here for the time being. At least we can fatten him up a bit. I want you to back me up with Mum on this. By the way, what are you doing here? No work today?"

"It's Easter Monday, Dad. Didn't the bunny bring you a chocolate egg yesterday?"

"Blimey, I forgot. Mum didn't say a word."

"Perhaps that's why she's gone to Aunt Peg's? Well, you've got time to make up for it. Get some flowers at least."

"I'd better if I want a quiet life. Go to the florist for me and get the biggest bunch of spring flowers they've got. There's a fist of pound notes in my wallet on the kitchen table. Please Joe, I've got to sort out this dog before Mum comes home. She's going to be doubly mad at me. Hang around; she won't commit murder in front of you." Although my wife was truly an animal lover, I was going to need to approach her with care. Timing was everything. Putting up with Barking-Bess was more than enough.

I found the towel, secured it tight around my waist. The garden was surrounded by a high wall so I was protected from any peeping tom and saved from being accused of indecent exposure. Bess was a bit sheepish when I went to get her from the garage. She had gnawed large splinters of wood off the door. She'd destroyed the back gate months ago, and the remaining one at the front was chewed to custom design with a perfect sized gap so she could challenge any passers-by. It was routine for the mailman to refuse delivery and threaten her annihilation with mace. "What am I going to do with you?" The concrete path was swept clean by her wagging tail and her mouth turned up in a cheery grin. She had me and knew it. Neither short nor longhaired, Bess was anything but an ordinary creature. Ears that were strong and straight became happy flaps, giving her a false docile impression. Her thick white coat and black almond eyes were clues to her Husky roots. She came to us as a pup over five years ago. Pretty much left on our doorstep. I really didn't want to keep her, what with long days at the factory, teenage kids, and a wife who needed a lot of attention. But once I saw how easily she fitted in with the family, and the effort she made to please, I knew I couldn't give her up. She became my devoted, forgiving pal. No matter what my mood, she'd be there at my side, instinctively reading me. Whenever I'd sit on the porch steps, it wouldn't be long before there'd be a wet, sticky nose teasing my hand to stroke her. Eventually, she'd fit her forty pounds onto my lap with a smug look declaring she had me fooled. I picked up her filthy spit-stained excuse for a ball and threw it for her; she skipped after it, delighted to have my attention and love back.

Joe returned with enough flowers to fill the kitchen sink; then he and I walked the neighbourhood to see if anyone had lost a dog or would like one. Despite our efforts, we came up blank, and my heart sank. When my wife returned, she saw the flowers but they did nothing to remove the scowl that appeared when she saw the new interloper. I promised I was working on finding a home for him but her scowl remained for the rest of the evening and the next few days. Joe didn't want him—needed to work more with his weights, he said; neither did our other kids, their excuses even less creative. It took a week before the retriever showed any sign of trust. When it felt safe, I let Bess meet him. There were a lot of sparks but they eventually settled their differences. Soon the weeks turned into months. My wife's pained expression seemed permanent, and got more so whenever I tried to get cosy.

I called the retriever Ben; it suited him. He grew from a dull rust colour to gold, with large intelligent eyes. He was a wonderful example of his breed and knew it. He and Bess coexisted under a contract drawn by Bess. With time, it became an equal partnership, and I found myself calmed by their presence. My wife eventually softened towards Ben. I'd catch her in the garden, deep in conversation with both dogs as she divided leftovers from dinner. I'm glad to say she softened towards me too.

Ben brought much to our lives; he was loyal and devoted, but a useless watchdog. It was as if he understood Bess handled that responsibility. He joyfully greeted everyone; carried the mail from the mailman, encouraged casual walkers to stop and pet him, and even managed to train Bess not to be so belligerent. It took a long time for him to have an influence over her barking, though. A long time. She continued her nightly performance and the neighbours' theirs. We even had a couple of visits from the police! Nothing seemed to deter her until, in the middle of a suicidal provoking sonata, Ben joined in. The racket was excruciating. I didn't just threaten to take both dogs to the pound, I had on my shoes and my car keys in hand. All of a sudden, the racket stopped—just like that—and was never to be heard again. Made me a believer, I can tell you. Our neighbours were just as dumbfounded, and became friendly again. Life has been blessed ever since.

I often look back on those days; they were such good ones. Ben liked nothing better than to walk in the park, carrying a toy in his large soft mouth or sitting quietly at my feet next to Bess. Bess became a different personality; more stable and content to be at Ben's side. I couldn't have wished for more devoted companions. We were together for many years, and I miss them. Of course, you've likely guessed. These two critters here, at my feet, are their offspring from a set of four. Funny looking aren't they? One white, the other golden. Their almond eyes, snub noses, and all that feathering down their legs explain their mixed pedigree. We call them Bess and Ben too.

HOT WATER CRIMES

...in other words, getting into trouble, right? I have certainly not lived a flat-line existence and have burnt myself much too often, albeit, for the most part, innocently. Having parents who demonstrated an abundance of discipline, one would think my two brothers and I straying from the straight and narrow was unlikely. That was a fantasy, of course. Now, with hindsight from an almost adult's perspective, I understand my safe *all things bright and beautiful* world was my own creation. I learned my brothers also created a fantasy in which to reside. As youngsters, the temperature of the water in which we found ourselves too often depended chiefly on our father's mood. The angrier he became the deeper the crimson his face became, and sweat poured out of every pore. He would bend over us as he raged, and we felt the heat of that sweat on our own brow. He never physically punished us but there were times when our flesh poached to burgundy from his harsh words.

Being of the *everything nice* gender, the reaction to any of my misdemeanours was tepid in comparison to my brothers'; however, I could have been raised to their level of heat when I stole a book of punch-out paper dolls. I'd desperately wanted one so I could play with my friend Lena. She received one for her birthday the week before. The glamorous clothing was fitted by means of paper tags that folded over the doll's shoulders. At eight years old, the temptation was too much for me when I saw what I greatly coveted was placed perfectly for easy pickings in the corner general shop. I was sent on the errand to buy a loaf of bread. I paid for the bread, and lingered in front of the display rack for a few moments. With no sense of wrongdoing that I can remember, I simply picked up a copy. No one stopped me; no one shouted "thief". I calmly walked out with both bread and book, and made my way home.

Lena came over to play later and brought her paper dolls book. She didn't question I had my own copy now. We were sitting on the stairs setting up a fashion show when my mother passed by. "How pretty your dolls look, Lena? So do those." She pointed to my collection and picked up a paper tennis dress. "Where did you get this?" I boldly replied, "I took it". "Did you pay for it?" I shook my head. "So you robbed the shopkeeper?" I looked at her for a moment. Her accusation stunned me. Robbed the shopkeeper? My tardy insight overruled my apathy. My eyes filled but Lena's were full of admiration. At that moment, a man's loud voice was heard in the distance. "Well, that was quick." Mother said. "They've traced you already. Did you hear your name?" I panicked, and grabbed her arm.

"Please don't let them take me away, Mummy." I struggled to breathe as sobs jammed in my throat.

"She didn't mean any harm." Faithful Lena pleaded as her face too began to crumble.

Mother told me to quickly put the dolls, clothing and remains of the book together in a bag. Holding my hand firmly, she took me to the street to wait for a car to drive passed our house. The car was large, and decorated with blue and white streamers and posters of a smiling man.

"Excuse me," Mother called, "my daughter has something to say to you." The driver must have been startled to see us on the curb, and he brought the car to a standstill. Mother gently urged her trembling daughter forward.

"I'm very sorry I stole this book." I handed him the bag.

There must have been some silent communication from my mother. He asked if I would do such a thing again. I tearfully assured him I was completely reformed. "I sincerely hope so. As long as you've learned a lesson, I will let it go this time, but if it happens again, your mother will let me know." Mother nodded her agreement.

I lived with fear that Father would find out, for I knew I would experience a dousing of very hot water for such a crime. My shame forced me well out of my way to complete any future errand I was cautiously entrusted with. I avoided neighbours, convinced they knew of my wicked deed, even though no red letter blazed on my chest. I clung to Lena, my champion, who told me in no uncertain terms to get over it. Eventually, I did, but there was residue of guilt because I never went back to the corner shop again. A few years later Mother was reminiscing about my childhood, and the incident came up.

"I shall never forget when you took the paper doll book. The conservative Parliamentary candidate came along at just the right moment. *Vote for me*, he kept calling out through the loud speaker, but I told you he was calling for you. You swallowed it hook line and sinker."

"I was only eight, Mummy. I had terrifying nightmares over it." My heart quickened with the memory.

"I'm sure you did, but you never again took anything without paying."

"No, never! And I appreciated you not telling Father."

"Yes, you can be thankful for that."

My two elder brothers were enrolled in grammar school where corporate punishment was part of the curriculum. One brother received a whack from a cane for inflicting stings on other students via stretched rubber bands. Those boys accepted it stoically as retaliation for their own tortures, but the house master thought he would get one up on all of them and names were reported to the headmaster. My brother admitted the resulted welts on his tender hand left painful swelling, but it was preferred to a verbal scolding if Father found out. Unfortunately, Father learned of the escapade via a sealed note from the school. Father's raised voice escaping through the door, made it clear my brother experienced a blistering dunking too.

Two years later both brothers graduated to college and I joined the grammar school, eventually became a prefect and then head girl. I was given the responsibility of persuading students to walk slowly along the halls and not push anyone down the stairs as they rushed to classes or the cafeteria. I was hardly successful, and wrote many up for detention. No one minded attending my Friday after-school sessions. Instead of duplicating the same quotation from Shakespeare's Tempest for ninety minutes, I introduced them to Miles Davis and Dave Brubeck. Word got out, of course. Although I never hid the fact, I was duly enlightened by Mr. Clark, a stern house master, that detentions were designed to reform unacceptable behaviour. I tried to make a case for my approach; indeed, I arrogantly thought if anyone took the time to do the research, they would have discovered those troublemakers in my care became jazz enthusiasts, and had no farther interest in disrupting the smooth running of our learning establishment. My dissertation was unsuccessful, and resulted in my hand stinging for hours and hot tears spilling from my eyes while I hid in the girls' shower room. Mother dealt with me which meant the temperature of the water I found myself in was considerably lower than that my brothers experienced.

Mr. Clark eventually came to one of my detentions. I felt deep resentment as remnants of pain psychologically returned to my hand and ego. I tried to ignore him sitting at the back tapping his foot to April in Paris by Charlie Parker with Strings. The dozen students didn't care one bit. They were in a different world...rolling in their seats to some of the greatest improvisation the Bird ever made. At the end of the session, Mr. Clark joined others looking through my limited record collection. I said nothing. The next morning in the middle of my desk was a 45rm record of Buddy Rich's Big Band. No note was attached. I played Buddy at home that evening and immediately became a fan.

I was stunned when I saw Father in the sitting room enjoying the hip music escaping from my room. He was tapping his fingers in time on the arm of his chair. I watched for a full minute, not believing my eyes. My brothers and I were already baffled over recent efforts from both parents to encourage not only our company but conversation too. What was going on? We decided to be prepared for something serious. Over dinner that evening, Father lamented we were growing up too quickly, and much time had been wasted in discord. Yes, he really did say discord. My brothers and I remained silent but welcomed his apparent awakening to our significance.

I was helping Mother with dinner dishes later, and asked what had brought on Father's more approachable demeanour. She smiled. "He wants things to change. He's trying to reach out, to show the love he's kept locked away from you children."

"How very strange." I stared at her, uncomprehending such a comment. "Why? Didn't he want us?"

"Oh, yes. He wanted you very much. We are well aware of the strain in the household, and what suffering it has caused—and it's going to stop."

"But why? Why has Father been so distant, so angry? And you, Mother, why have you allowed it?"

"Father and I went through a tragedy that changed everything for us. We should have explained ourselves a long time ago but it was too painful to bring up."

"Yes, Mother, you should have *explained yourselves*! We most certainly deserve that. It is time we knew why we've lived such a walking on egg-shells existence. Father is unapproachable; a punishing tyrant. It has been unbearable." I was angry...and deeply hurt. "How do you lock away love? That's sick."

She sat down at the table, and clasped her hands together. "Yes, it is sick, and it has brought Father and me to a breaking point many times." She paused to take in a breath. "I can only imagine what it has done to you children." She looked at me for a moment, and then continued quietly. "You had an older sister. She was our first child and we called her Sunny because that was what she was. She brought so much joy, and was particularly close to Grandfather; he visited almost daily to be with her after Grandmother died. She would watch for him by the window. One afternoon, she slipped out of the house when she saw his car and ran out into the car's path. Grandfather didn't see her in time, and she was killed. She was three." Mother's lip trembled.

"We had a sister?" I accused. "A sister? Why would you keep such a thing from us?" I had no sympathy, only fury.

"Losing her sent us into the depths of despair. The weight of remorse caused Grandfather to decline quickly. When he died we were certain it was from a broken heart. Father entered into a psychiatric hospital for a few weeks. I was pregnant with your eldest brother, and somehow that kept me sane." Her voice was a whisper. "Father's grief has held him prisoner ever since; it has kept him from those he loves."

"If he loves us, why does he treat us so harshly, made us afraid of him? What did we have to do with anything? We're not bad children. The boys and I try hard to stay out of what we call Father's hot water, because it feels like we're plunged up to our necks into the heat of his rage too often."

"That won't be happening again, I promise you. It's so very complicated, darling. I know it sounds odd but his anger is against himself because he holds himself responsible for Sunny's death and Grandpa's suffering. He is drowning in hot water too, as you put it— at times he cannot breathe. His frequent angry outbursts at you and your brothers guarantee detachment from him. It pushes you away but it punishes him deeply. The psychiatrist told us self-punishment reduces those terrible feelings of guilt, and frees our conscience to allow us to reengage in life. It's so strange. I struggled to understand but at some level it seems so. He knows what it does to you. As I said, it is complicated."

"Why would Father be guilty?"

"He was reading the newspaper and didn't notice Sunny leave the room and run out to Grandpa. He cannot forgive himself and is tortured by despair."

"Are we going to live like this for ever?"

"No. If Father doesn't make the effort to change as promised, I will leave him and you children will come with me. It is up to him now. He knows he has a lot of making up to do. We both have. I recognise my part and I am very sorry for it. I hope the three of you will allow us that chance."

"It is too much to take in. Fear shouldn't be between a father and his children. Why now? Why is he willing to reach out now?"

"Simply because he cannot cope any more. His sanity rests in letting go and showing up as a loving father to his living children.

"I don't know if I love him any more. Do you?"

"I love him so very much." She covered her face with her hands and wept.

"Oh, Mother." I got up and put my arms around her. I could not remember seeing her cry before, and my heart ached as I acknowledged her pain. As her tears flowed so did mine.

"What's going on?" Father stood at the door. I noticed how gaunt he was. A flush of sorrow and love came over me.

"Father, I know about Sunny." I watched his face crumble as he came over to Mother and me with his arms open wide.

We had a meeting that evening. My brothers discharged some heated words. They demanded to know how to approach an unapproachable father. Father's anger erupted defensively, and we felt little sympathy as he struggled for control. The next couple of weeks were very difficult. We were reticent with each other, but as more time passed, the awkwardness became less. Eventually, Father was able to talk about the pain that had held him captive for so long. It was a heart wrenching experience for all of us, but the more he talked, the better we all felt. Eventually things settled down, mainly because emotional exhaustion took over. When Father and Mother asked for forgiveness we knew a paradigm change had taken place. The crimes that had put us into such hot water were laughable from a distance, although my brothers and I saw nothing laughable about what we went through over them. We talked and talked; all the pent-up feelings just exploded from each of us. It wasn't easy but it felt good. It took a longer time for Father to thaw. Family and individual counselling helped a lot. I sometimes felt so sad, I couldn't stop crying. That heart breaking secret had robbed us of so much, but we are on a new path now where we have discovered real love for the father who has returned to us. We enjoy energised dialogue over dinner, an occasional trip to the cinema or quietly reading in the same room. Nothing earth shattering but giant steps for us. When my brothers are home at weekends, Father often takes them to a local football game. Their boisterous enthusiasm when the team wins is contagious. We visit Sunny's gravesite, and make sure there are plenty of flowers around. Our big sister is real to us now. Looking back, it was as if strings that were pulled tight on a bundle of emotions were suddenly released.

My school had an open house recently, and I was proud to introduce Mother and Father to staff and students. I am graduating soon but intend continuing my detention sessions until the big day. The music and fellowship allowed me to escape from the trauma at home. My fellow jazz enthusiasts let me be, and their kindness is tucked in my heart. My record collection increased considerably, thanks to not only Father, and now includes two of his favourites— the scat singing of Ella Fitzgerald and the wondrous voice of Sarah Vaughan. He often takes my brothers and me to HMV, the world's largest music shop on Oxford Street that was opened in 1921 by the composer Sir Edward Elgar. One can get just about any piece of music, recorded or otherwise, and the sales assistant somehow knows exactly where to find it in that massive space. It really is massive, and we explore each of its three floors for hours before meeting Mother for tea at a local café. Mr. Clark continues to turn up often on Fridays; my hostility toward him faded long ago. His rank is forgotten when he spends time talking about his own love of modern jazz. He and Father have become acquainted, well enough to enjoy an occasional lunch or a pint together at the local pub. When I showed Father a waiting list of those who went out of their way to cause enough ruckus to qualify for my Friday detentions, he was most impressed.

He put his arm around my shoulders while students gathered around us, eager to brag they had begun their own jazz clubs that met after school or at weekends. He told them about his own love of the music, and thrilled us all with his rendering of Fascinating Rhythm on the corner piano. My love for him brought me to tears.

It was with amusement I watched those students walking through the corridors on my last day. Music had become a part of many of them; so much so, few could walk without their heads nodding and a beat to their step. When instrument cases were being carried along with school satchels, everyone knew Sloan Square Grammar School was the groovy place to be. Oh, such happy days! Miles, Dave, Charlie, Buddy, Ella, Sarah and the rest of you incredible music makers—thank you. You not only put rhythm in our souls, but helped a wounded family find its way.

LIFE IS EVERY WHERE

I was sitting on the back doorstep reading my mail and enjoying an early morning cup of tea. It had been a foggy night, and the garden glistened with heavy dew. My bones absorbed the warmth turned up by the sun. I wriggled my toes in pleasure and gazed about me. A small plane droned above, towing a streamer announcing life was unliveable without a certain type of shampoo. On my right a tiny blue tit (Parus caeruleus) was hanging upside down breakfasting on greasy grubs from a foxglove's purple spear of flowers. Every now and then, it held its head back to examine the foliage for additional tasty bites. From my peripheral view, I became aware of another movement. I turned my head, and faced a large web. It seemed deceivingly fragile, as if it would collapse from the weight of many dewdrops shimmering like tiny prisms filled with rainbows; in the centre was a large orange spider flexing its many legs, perhaps to awaken circulation after a chilly night, just like many of us. I had read scientists were working to combine the DNA of spider silk with that of the silk worm to produce a thread that will be virtually unbreakable. The Smithsonian reported artificial spider silk was in the works.

I used to have a phobic horror of these creatures. It was impossible for me to open any journal if I thought it contained photographs of those creepy creatures, but wonder had nudged out my repulsion and I watched spellbound. The spider suddenly dropped from its perch, and safely anchored by its thread, swung to a branch of neighbouring shrubbery and disappeared. With the architect away, I was able to focus on its creation. The web was like intricately worked lace—a "best" doily to place on a silver tray to serve a special treat, but no skilled hands of a Brussels' matron were involved with this masterpiece. Memories leaked back from biology classes, and I recalled how each individual section of the web is shaped: the most difficult part being the first thread, for that needs the collaboration of a breeze to transport it to a spot where it can anchor, and form the first bridge. Once this bridge is reinforced, a loose thread is constructed to make a Y shape, becoming the first of three radii of the web. A frame is then formed to attach the other two. The web is completed when the last sticky thread is woven around and between all the radii. This web had twenty-one. I looked in awe at the remarkable design—and wondered what an ancient eye might have thought while standing in my place. Later, forgetting the occupant in the bushes, I walked straight into the web spread at eye level across the walkway. Who has not experienced stumbling into the sticky netting that adheres to the face, and danced a frantic jig to claw it off? I felt quite guilty for causing so much repair work for this tiny being.

Spring became summer. A couple of good-natured cats visited from time to time, and a variety of birds took up residence and I knew there was at least one residing Aranea. Weeks later, I was on the patio filling planters with pansies, when a loud squawking broke through my placidity. I squinted through one eye to observe the creature that had so intrusively broken my concentration. It was a large black and white bird. This particular specimen, however, had a wing trailing as he tried to compete with the ever present sparrows for the crumbs I had scattered earlier. I stood silently to give him a chance to get used to my presence. He watched cautiously as I walked towards him and cowered when I carefully picked him up and held the broken appendage against his pounding chest. He turned his head and observed me with luminous black eyes. "I'll take care of you." I assured him. I felt he believed me.

I caught the bus at the end of the street. "Animals up top, miss", the conductor announced cheerfully. I made my way up the narrow stairs and seated myself in the back, fully aware of the large Alsatian dog taking up most of the aisle three seats down. I ventured a peek into my coat and was utterly charmed by the small intelligent face that popped up, and I found myself talking gently to reassure it, as if to a child.

"What you got there, luv'?" A red face in need of a shave turned around from the seat in front. "That's a bleeding magpie, ain't it?" His Cockney accent was grating. "It's tame, then?"

"No. I just found it in the garden. I think its wing's broken so I'm taking it to the vet."

"Poor little geezer."

By this time, other passengers were inquisitive about what I had tucked in my coat, and a few moved to the seats around me.

"It's a wild bird. Show it to us, miss." A couple of uniformed schoolboys, satchels dragging, squeezed into the seat across from me. I couldn't respond because there was a struggle going on inside my coat. I hastily tried to fasten the top button but, too late, the small black head emerged, followed by skinny shoulders.

"Oh, Mummy, look." A small girl pulled at her mother's arm.

The bird climbed out from my coat and positioning itself on my shoulder. It looked from side to side at its fascinated audience, and settled itself down. It seemed to review the situation with alert shining eyes, enjoying all the attention.

"Come on now; back in your seats." The conductor gently ushered those standing around me, and I was thankful to see we had arrived at our destination.

The veterinarian's assistant was very kind and put the bird into a comfortable cage.

"What's his name?"

"What?"

"His name—what do you call him?"

"Oh, I just found him in my garden. He's wild." I was trying to remove the considerable dirt from the lining of my coat with my handkerchief, and was in no mood to delay returning home.

"Well, he's got to have a name—I need to put one on the card."

"It's a boy, then?" I looked at her with not a trace of humour. "Very well. Mike Magpie."

She actually wrote it down.

The vet expertly manipulated the iridescent wing feathers and ran his fingers over the matted body. "Broken wing for sure. Tell me what happened."

"I don't know. I found Mike, um, him—the bird, in my garden. I could see he was hurt."

"He'll have to stay for a couple of weeks. I'll set the wing, and keep my eye on him. Trusting little bugger, isn't he."

"What'll happen to him when he's better?"

"We'll let him go. Should be able to fend for himself just fine. If we put him in the park, there'll be plenty of people to oblige with a daily meal or two."

About a month or so later, he was perched on the wall, looking sleek and alert. Both wings were tight against the sides of his plump white chest and the black feathers shone with a radiant blue. I was overjoyed to see him looking so well. I sat down on the grass and looked up at him. "Hello, Mike. How are you doing?" He didn't even flutter his wings but hopped down in front of me. It wasn't long before he climbed up on my lap and started to peck at the shiny button on my cardigan. As he became more confident, he tucked his head inside, and the rest of him quickly followed. Magpies are large birds, and there wasn't much room, yet it felt right somehow to have him stuffed there, and I felt immense pleasure to see him again.

Later, I was able to sketch a few quick studies of this arresting creature. He was about eighteen inches, with a long iridescent tail. His black head, breast, back and rump were striking against his white belly. But it was his brilliantly alive eyes that held me. There was wisdom, experience, deep in those black beads, and he had a habit of holding his head to one side as our gaze locked into each other. I was much moved by him. He stayed around for a week before disappearing, and I watched anxiously, hoping for his return. I made sure the birdbath was full and seed plentiful from then on. But he didn't come back.

I hadn't given much thought to the spider for quite a while, and went over one morning to see how she'd fared now we were passed summer's end. The web looked in bad shape but I knew after a night of hunting, the web can get worn out. However, I saw no sign of life. Spiders remove most broken silk in the mornings, usually leaving the first bridge line, and then they rest for the remainder of the day. Any repair work is done during the evening, and then the trap is set again. My spirit sank. I'd lost Mike, and now this creature.

It was early evening when I took out a pile of newspapers to the trash bin. The light from the porch reflected on a perfect new web strung across its claimed territory; the shadow was a line drawing against the wall in the deepening twilight. The spider was positioned in the middle, ready for the hunt. Several flying insects were heading in her direction, and I knew her larder would be stocked before the chill became cold and her food supply became scarce. I thought of Mike. Where was he now? Had he flown off to a far distant place to set up house with an affectionate mate now an autumn tone had begun to touch the land? I had no answers, of course, and reflected on the two amazing beings I'd had the good fortune to meet. What else lay "out there"? For sure, I would be watching.

On a crisp morning I was doing my best to dig up a couple of privet bushes that had succumbed to a very harsh winter. I took off my muddy gloves and was in the midst of a good back stretch when I saw a magpie watching from the wall. I held my breath. "Mike? Mike, is that you?" I walked over to him and sat on the grass. He hopped from the wall and stood in front of me. He looked sleek, his white chest plump "It is you, isn't it? I'm so glad to see you again." I stretched out my hand but he backed away, uncertain. Then he flew off. With feelings of both elation and disappointment, I went back to tackling the bushes.

Exhausted, I barely had the energy to put the tools away. The pile of branches and roots were in the bin, and the ground was turned over ready for new plantings. I was pleased with myself; actually, rather proud. I sat on the step by the back door and took off my filthy boots. It was then that I saw him perched on the back of a wrought iron chair. "Hello, Mike." He was uncertain and seemed about to fly off. I slowly walked to the chair and sat down, keeping silent and still. After a moment, I began talking softly, bringing him up to date with the goings on in the neighbourhood. His intelligent beady eyes looked intently into mine as he listened with his head on one side. I stroked his silk-like feathers, and he leaned into me. Pleasure overfilled my heart.

A full year has passed now. Another spring is over, and Mike has returned again. In fact, he is sitting on my shoulder at this moment. Neighbours are used to us now, their puzzled stares are long gone; when I take a stroll with Mike perched on my shoulder or peering out of my coat, they just smile and wave. When his internal clock tells him it is time, his strong wings take him away to places only he knows but I am not dismayed. My Mike will return after a fling or two, and perhaps one day he will bring a wife...and maybe a couple of kids to meet me. It's not impossible, is it?

ONCE UPON A TIME

"Got a couple of dollars for coffee, honey?" Three men sat on the wall surrounding my employer's guest parking. Winter in California is seldom harsh but it was bitterly cold and wet that morning. I opened my purse with stiff fingers. Yes, there was a ten dollar bill. I handed it over; annoyed it was a ten instead of a five and by the direct solicitation. I looked into the unshaven red face of a man about fifty years old. Sparse hair was plastered against his uncovered head. He wore no jacket, just a navy sweatshirt that was heavy with rain. He nodded, touching my hand as he took the bill. "Thanks a lot. We need a warm up." I was relieved to get to my office, and made a beeline for the kitchen to pour my own cup of hot coffee and gratefully helped myself from the box of muffins a kind colleague had brought in. "Hey, Barb—delicious," I called out. I hung up my wet coat, and settled down to deal with the papers piled on my desk. My office felt cosy, and I soon thawed out. By lunchtime, my appetite had developed, and I decided a bowl of soup and grilled sandwich from the convenient in-house cafeteria would hold me over until dinner that evening.

About a week later I saw the same three men sitting on the same wall. I absently returned their smile as they wished me a good day. I was soon sipping on a hot coffee at my desk, reviewing several pages of items that required my resolute attention. Gradually, the outside world evaporated from my consciousness, and, without realizing it, I...the me...vanished into the confined sterile space too. I became an

89

American citizen after emigrating from Europe ten years ago, and had worked for the same company since then, gradually climbing the ladder of success. "Good for you," my colleagues smiled, shaking my hand warmly. That was what I thought, until I was moved to a small windowless space with a computer and telephone, and a work load that became insurmountable.

The company's employee parking structure was a couple of blocks away, and my assigned space was on the top level. We were currently experiencing particularly bad weather and a few daring employees were sneaking into the more convenient lot of the historic red brick town hall. I was about to join them just as the City's parking attendants caught on. The hefty fines incurred deterred that idea from developing, and I remained at the parking structure. Fortunately, the walk to the office was not a problem most of the time. On one particularly wet morning, I was waiting at a traffic light to cross the road when a strong gust of wind grabbed my umbrella. I stood stupefied as it flew along the road and bounced off several cars crawling along in the heavy torrent. The rain ran through my hair, down my neck, and seeped into the collar of my favourite green blouse my raincoat was supposed to protect.

I looked and felt pretty sorry for myself when I reached the office building. The three men were huddled under heavy tarpaulins, dry but as miserable as me. I hurried passed as usual, but when I got to my desk, I became full of anxiety. I just stared at the files and notes while shivering. After a few moments, I pulled on my wet raincoat, grabbed someone's umbrella that was dripping in a waste bin, and hurried out. I had a surge of elation that took away the chill creeping along my own spine as I self-consciously placed the bags from the local McDonald's on the wall beside the men and hurried on. Later, on the way to pick up my car, I saw the empty paper cups and wrappers neatly folded and tucked into a corner of the garden landscape by the wall.

I didn't see them for a couple of weeks; then they were in their reserved seats again. "Have a good one, honey." The man looked stiff with cold. I turned and made for McDonald's.

"Breakfast." I held out several paper bags. The men looked at me, expressionless. "There's some cash for hot food and a shower at the YMCA. I phoned over there and learned you can get a change of clothes too."

"Miss, it's really kind of you, but we're okay—certainly not your problem."

"You don't understand. I'm not okay and I won't be okay until you get going. My boss will be wondering where I am."

They stared at me, uncertain, and then got off the wall. "Thank you. We won't forget this." The man was about sixty and well worn by life. They shuffled away, looked back and waved.

Whenever I saw them after that, I tried to provide at least a cup of coffee and a few dollars, but I began to worry. The amount I was spending soon added up and I had difficulty keeping to my budget, but I was committed. When a couple of co-workers noticed I wasn't buying lunch from the cafeteria any more, they asked if I was all right. I assured them I was; said I was simply saving the money. Apparently, word got around because a sandwich and drink began to appear from the cafeteria each day; apparently on orders from my boss. Then anonymous envelopes containing cash were put on my desk. I didn't know who was responsible so I took a length of paper towels from the kitchen and taped a giant thank you message on the wall so it was seen when the envelope delivery person opened my office door. I was feeling really uneasy taking the cash and decided to come clean with my boss about what I was doing. He thought it appropriate my co-workers knew how their money was being spent, then they could decide what they wanted to do. I was red faced when I approached them but they were most supportive, and agreed to continue supplementing my activities; at least for a while.

The extra money allowed for the breakfast menu to change from time to time, and occasionally to include warm sweaters, jackets and gloves that I got at bargain prices from the Goodwill Industries shop down the road a-ways, and I accounted for every cent I spent. I tried to be sensitive about how I handed over the items. I knew the men had pride and I didn't want to bruise that. Usually, I leaned the bags against the railing by the wall and said nothing. It was pure guesswork getting sizes that worked but I don't think they minded if a sleeve was a little long or the colour wasn't a favourite. Eventually, we became easy with each other. As the weather warmed, I began leaving home earlier in the morning so I could sit on the wall with them, sipping on my own cup of coffee. The geraniums in the company landscaping began to open. The wall absorbed the sun's rays and it became a more agreeable place for our gatherings.

Over the following months, I learned about the suffering each man had endured while trying to survive on the streets. They'd been in the struggle for a long time, joining the homeless sprawl around the Civic Centre grounds for their place of residence. Eventually there was room for a couple of nights at the men's homeless shelter on Main Street. It was there the three met, and decided to watch out for each other once back on the streets. I listened without interrupting. I no longer saw their shabby clothes, the dirt under their fingernails; instead, I heard the ache in their voices, the fear they would never get on their feet again. One told me about his eight-year old all-legs daughter—the age when he last saw her. She was now twelve, and he feared they would lose contact. "How can I show up like this?" His eyes filled and so did mine. Another talked about his fight with the demons of alcohol but proudly announced his sobriety of three weeks. "These guys help me," he said simply. I listened without judgment, aware only of their honesty and the loyal camaraderie between them. They asked a few questions of me: my name, where was I from and what kind of work I did? And why wasn't I married?

Occasionally, a middle-aged woman dressed in well-worn purple sweats and lace-less high-top tennis shoes would walk by. Our friendly greetings were ignored. She was in the midst of an animated conversation with a real person to her but invisible to the rest of us; presumably it was an enjoyable tête-à-tête because she was smiling. We watched her turn the corner. Richard, the father, voiced the question on our minds: who looks out for her? In spite of the daily hardships the three men endured, they had the good fortune of support from each other. A couple of days later, I went out to run errands during my lunch hour. The woman was standing on the street corner. Although the sun was out, she was rubbing her hands together, trying to keep warm. The wind was up, and quite raw—enough to make me button up my wool jacket. She walked towards me as I got closer to her, then she abruptly turned and quickly walked away. Her figure kept breaking into my thoughts while I tried to study a report later, and I added her to my worry list. Where did she sleep? Did she get enough to eat? A newly built women's shelter was due to open in a few months, thanks to financing by local businesses that included my employer. In the meantime, what do such women do until then?

When I left home that next morning, I took along a heavy knit cardigan a friend had given me as a birthday present the year before. I had never worn it; not only was it too big for me, the many colours would have challenged Joseph's coat those centuries ago. I tucked into the pockets a red woollen hat and scarf, and a pair of thick gloves. Inside one glove, I folded a couple of dollars. I carried that bundle back and forth for over two weeks before I saw her again. She was sitting on "our" wall, talking up a storm to her invisible companion. I sat beside her. She was younger than I thought, her hair had a natural curl and was blond under the grime; and she was pretty. "Hello," I said cheerfully. She got up, and quickly walked away.

I kept that cardigan in my car for about a month until I saw her emerging from behind a large dumpster. This receptacle was not only a rubbish container but had evolved into a unisex public convenience too. I'd be late for work, but didn't care—I was on a mission. I ran back to my car and grabbed the bundle. Eventually, I caught up with her. As usual, she was raving, and oblivious of me trying to block her path. I stepped in front of her and put the cardigan on the ground. "This is for you," I said loudly, and walked away. Did she understand? Would she accept my offering, or would some passer-by pick it up? I walked slowly to the car park after work that day, disappointed there was no sign of her, or the cardigan. It wasn't until the following week when I saw the wildly coloured cardigan and red woollen hat moving along in the distance. I was so happy, I actually whooped aloud. The woman was walking at her usual pace, arms flaying as she made her point, but I swear her step had a swagger.

Almost a year passed before I changed my job location. About six month before then, Richard, Clive and Bob, those three extraordinary men, moved on. I didn't know where. They just didn't show up one morning, and never returned again. I missed them so and, of course, worried about them. It took a while for me to process our coming together. My initial resentment of the street people could easily have been a barrier to knowing wonderful individuals who showed me only respect and friendship. How quickly I judged them: *blight on society, lazy, dirty, druggies, bums! Why don't they get a job—the rest of us have to*? I am grateful for the chance to rethink such opinions. I still smile when I remember a woeful young man who stopped me one morning. "I was a bad boy last night, drank too much and the police took my car. I'm asking five people for two dollars each for the bus fare so I can get home" He looked embarrassed but resolute. "Can you help me?" Did he tell me the truth? I chose to think so.

"I'm not sure I have any cash," I said, opening my purse. Right on top were two new crisp one dollar bills. I looked at him, he looked at me. "Obviously, yours." Of course, they were.

"God and my wife bless you, miss. Four more people to go. I hope I make it." His step was a little unsteady as he hurried along.

Such simple get-togethers brought me what I needed, but that insight was unknown to me at the time. I gratefully look at my life differently now and regularly share the abundance I enjoy. I have the freedom and access to whatever it takes to fulfil my basic needs. When I'm thirsty—I drink. When I'm cold I put on a warm sweater, and each night I curl up in a comfortable bed. I took all that for granted. Now I know I could easily become one of those *lazy bums,* losing my sense of self in the labelling if my own earning capacity ceased. My encounters, particularly with three gentle men and one fragile butterfly enriched my life and opened my eyes. I know I am not the only one but it takes only one to make a difference. Collectively, I learned miracles can happen, and one did.

PORTRAIT

She leaned over the damp embankment overlooking the meandering River Arno, and reached out her hand and broke the surface of the cool water. Her reflection revealed a robust young woman of around seventeen with explosions of blue and silver highlights in her long black hair, and a skin turned to nut brown by the harsh summer sun. She wore a simple gown of homespun wool—no clever stitch to decorate—splatters of mud were its adornment. The water lapping against the algae-covered stones seemed to hypnotize her. Thick like good stock, the water furrowed gently, stroked by a spirited breeze. Minutes passed peacefully, and she imagined herself far away from the noise and smells of Arezzo, a small village nestled amongst olive and walnut trees in the rural Tuscan landscape.

It took effort for Francesca Bellini to return to the reality of her gruelling life. Reluctantly, she dried her hands on her apron while observing loaded donkeys scurrying on bone-thin legs along the cobblestone path. Local merchants sang out with melodious voices to market their fruits and vegetables, household wares and richly coloured cloth. Francesca caught sight of her younger sister Maria, and ran to greet her. With arms draped around each other, they made off to complete the purchases entrusted to them by their mother.

Lorenzo and Subette Bellini were simple peasants who worked the land with hands gnarled and twisted like the roots they fought deep in the cool soil. Set against ancient trees, their home was a dark thatched hut. Dust kicked up from the dirt floor by the constant movement of children and animals was ripe with pungent odours that pervaded the air. The day was warm, and the hut was over-heated by the evening meal boiling in a large pot over a wood fire. Francesca and Maria arrived with their purchases, and the younger children excitedly demanded to know the contents of the bundles they carried. Subette scurried away the noisy youngsters; she was eager to get on with the final preparations for the family's one substantial meal of the day.

The vegetables and remains of a rabbit snared days ago were eaten ravenously; the last drop of gravy soaked up by hot crusty bread. Subette chided Lorenzo over the unsavoury flavour of the onions. The root cellar was almost empty, and the vegetables that remained had soured and tasted of mildew. He reminded her of the new harvest ahead. Until then, they would have to make do. The winter of 1502 would not soon be forgotten. The weather had been more harsh than usual, and they had lost livestock as well as crops. Even their dwelling had suffered from the severity of the elements. Lashed by rain and sleet, the mud walls had crumbled in areas, and much of the sod roof had been lost to the winds. The country folk laboured to the point of exhaustion during the new year's spring planting. The coming summer's anticipated yield brought much hope to all of them.

The setting sun was a giant orange hovering on the dark blue horizon, transforming the lush landscape into obscure shadows. Plenty of chores remained, but dusk was Francesca's favourite time, and she often escaped from the sharp-eye of her mother for a few stolen minutes. A wooden cart parked by the dilapidated barn was filled with alfalfa. She climbed aboard, and lay back in its fragrance and relaxed. Birds returning to their nests for the night twittered and fussed as they settled. An occasional stomp resonated from the stall as the mule shifted weight from one leg to another. Her young brother, Carlos, his hair every-which-way and a dry mucus crust around his nostrils, peered over the side of the cart and shook Francesca from her lethargy. "You must return to the house immediately. A gentleman is with Mama and Papa and he wants to talk with you."

As Francesca hurried along, her bare callused feet scattered dew from the grass, and dampened her skirt. She paused at the door before entering the house to listen but the voice was unfamiliar. The elderly man made an impressive presence in his fine red brocade coat and black hat adorned with a pheasant feather and large ruby. His face, hiding behind a long unkempt beard and thick wiry eyebrows, was densely wrinkled like crepe. As he stepped forward to the candlelight, his piercing eyes shimmered like liquid topaz. Francesca curtsied as her father presented her.

"Come here, child," the stranger said, and roughly took her chin in his hand, turning her face from side to side. Francesca blushed from his close scrutiny, and glanced questioningly at her father.

"Daughter, this gentleman has noticed you in the village on several occasions. He is an artist, and wants to paint your portrait."

Francesca's eyes widened in surprise. "Why would you choose to paint me? I'm so plain, sire." Francesca voiced the question the family wanted to ask, but were too reticent to speak out. The stranger was obviously wealthy, and in their eyes, superior. He must be treated with the utmost respect, and that meant one held one's tongue.

"Yes, you are homely and your eyes are undersized, but I received a commission to paint a portrait of a young woman of my choice. I have decided to paint someone unknown, who will be presented in such a way as to arouse interest." He swept his hand in the air dramatically. "She will create a mystery. The public will crave to know who she is." He turned to Signor Bellini. "Rest assured, farmer, my name is known throughout Italy for many reasons beyond portrait painting. You can trust me, and I will pay well."

"How much?" Signora Bellini smiled coyly.

"This is my only offer." His voice was impatient as he wrote a figure in the dust on the table. "Can you read what I have written, peasant?"

"I understand. I learned to count in order to sell our produce at a profit." Signor Bellini looked at his wife and nodded.

"We will take your offer." Signora Bellini's eyes glistened at the thought of the many things the family needed. At the top of the list were the hut and barn roof repairs, shoes for everyone—and a new scythe. The list was long, but the artist's payment of many ducats would help shorten it considerably. She exchanged a smile with her husband who moved forward and sealed the contract with a bow.

"Girl, I shall expect you to be at my studio at daybreak on the morrow. I work early to catch the light. Do not be late." He handed Francesca a few coins. "Buy some perfumed soap and wash your hair. You can wear that dress, but I expect it, too, to be clean. My studio is at the side of the Ponte Due, the entrance is marked by a wooden sign with two blue plumes." He turned, and without another word, swept passed them out into the night

Francesca knocked timidly on the wooden door. Her heart quickened with apprehension.

"Come in, girl." The artist looked at her closely and saw her hair was freshly washed and her dress, although still damp, was dirt free. "Good—you are clean and on time." The artist wore a blue garment under a plain coverall of brown cloth splashed with paint of many colours. His head was uncovered. Long strands of grey hair intermingle with the side curls of his beard, and cascaded down his back. Francesca noticed his nails were well cared for. He led her into a large spacious room and Francesca breathed in air that was heavy with a scent she had not known before. There was little furniture to compete with canvases at various stages of completion propped against the walls. A long wooden table was laden with rolls of paper, some plain, while others had odd shapes and numbers drawn on them. Pots atop a small cabinet contained paintbrushes of many sizes, a muddle of chalks and engraving tools. An hourglass with an empty upper chamber, jostling for space with heavy jars filled with different pigments that had spilled to leave circles of brilliant colours. Francesca looked around in wonder.

The artist guided Francesca to an outside terrace where a white Persian cat and a greyhound dog were playing quietly together. He gestured towards a chair set between two tall stone columns.

"Sit there." Francisca did as she was told. "Fold your hands in your lap; turn your body slightly away from me. Yes, that's it. Now look back at me. No, child—that is too much. Look at me." His voice was abrupt, yet not abrasive. "Think of all the pleasures you have imagined. I want a soft mouth, a knowing mouth." The greyhound nuzzled Francesca's knee and she moved to stroke its noble head. "Stay in position, girl. You must not take your focus away from me." Francesca's lip trembled with nervousness. "I will sketch an outline first of all, and we must not talk for a while. It is important that you keep this pose during this period."

Francesca had been in the pose for only a short time before it seemed every muscle began to ache and cramps developed in her legs.

"Sire, I feel faint."

"You must do better than this or I will never finish," he admonished. Francesca rebelled at his insensitivity and was about to stand up. "Stop!" The artist shouted. "You must learn discipline."

"But I must move! My legs…they hurt so! And I'm cold!" Francesca's heart was beating rapidly and her hands were moist with anxiety.

"We will finish soon. Take your mind to a higher place, away from yourself and your aches!"

"I cannot! It is too much!"

The artist's temper flared, and he threw down the crayon in disgust. He took her arm roughly and led her back into the studio. "There!" He indicated a chair in the middle of the room where shafts of thin light came together and softened her features. Skin that was tanned and roughened by her hard life became smooth and her hair took on the richness of ebony. "Perhaps you will find it warmer, Signorina Bellini?" His tone was mocking.

Francesca's anxiety increased as the minutes ticked away but she remained in position. The crayon skating across the canvas was the only sound to interrupt the tense silence. Muscles cramped painfully in her legs but she said nothing. It seemed an eternity before the artists put down his crayon and straightened his back with a groan.

"That's enough for today. You can get up from the chair now."

Her legs were numb and she stumbled to the window to breathe in cool air from the river. The sun was high, and she squinted against the glare.

"Come, child, have some refreshment. You can then return to your family."

Francesca found the fruit delicious; the wine brought a blush to her cheeks and renewed her energy.

"When will I see what you have drawn?"

"Not until I have made the final brushstroke." He wiped his fingers thoroughly on a clean piece of rag to remove all particles of crayon. "I work fast but it will take a long time. A lot will depend on you. Always be on time, and you must stop complaining. The longer you sit, the quicker we shall be done." The artist touched her shoulder. "You have done well for the first day. We have a partnership, you and I. We are equals in the creation of this painting."

Francesca had not been spoken to in such a manner before. A partner? The stranger was speaking with her as if she was an equal—as if her contribution was just as important as his. She knew she was loved deeply but it would never occur to anyone in her family to acknowledge her in such a way. The focus revolved around where the next meal was coming from, how to earn more cash. She was no more than the eldest daughter and accepted it.

"I'll be back tomorrow, on time. And will sit so still you will wonder." Her cheeks flushed with pleasure, conveying more than any words how jubilant she felt. The artist's smile was soft as she slipped away.

"You have plenty to make up for after being gone so much."

"Si, Mama—I will."

Francesca picked up the broom and went into combat with the dirt floor, shooing a couple of clucking chickens as she hurried around the small room. Heat from the wood fire released scent from bundles of rosemary and thyme hanging from the rafters; they sweetened the air and helped lift her spirit.

The days were long but Francesca washed her hair and dress each evening with the perfumed soap, as she had promised the artist. She sat close to the fire to dry her hair while the thick wool dress steamed and filled the room with the stench of animal oil. Exhaustion soon took over, until her eyes refused to remain open and she fell into a restful sleep, awakening to the first light and cold ashes in the grate. The artist's attitude was softening towards her. Meticulous about his own hygiene, he was pleased she arrived clean and fresh each morning, ensuring the stink and grime of the farm were kept out of his studio. "You are doing well," he told her, and his own confidence grew. She looked up at him, and their eyes met in mutual respect. "I have a surprise for you, child. The cat and dog are only distractions so I have arranged for musicians to play for you each day. They will keep you entertained while I work and allow me to progress more quickly." Francesca was thrilled. And so a routine was established. Francesca slept in front of the fire each night, too exhausted to pull herself to the cot she shared with Maria. She had become used to wearing clean clothing and bathing each day but it set her apart from her siblings, and feelings became strained between them. She was becoming an outcast.

She arrived early each morning at the house by the side of the Ponte Due, and enjoyed the escape from her narrow life. Occasionally, a poet would recite a poem or read passages from books. Francesca did not understand the words but enjoyed the rhythm of the sounds. Six musicians played music that eventually became familiar to her, and she hummed the melodies while working at the farm. As he worked, the artist became talkative. He explained about linseed oil, ground pigment and other materials he was using for the portrait, and that he would use a cottonwood panel instead of a canvas to extend the preservation of the work. He explained how nature and the whole spectrum of life intrigued him, from the movement of crabs to the growth patterns of trees, and described some of the ideas he had explored while a younger man. Francesca listened intently; her imagination developing until she, too, believed man would one day ride in flying machines and swim under water for several minutes because of a sack of air affixed to a special suit. One morning, the master showed her his "glasses": two pieces of polished glass held within a wire frame that wrapped around his ears, and with which he could see and sketch the moon.

Francesca came to love and respect the scholarly man with large brown eyes. Eventually, their relationship changed and they became like father and daughter. She found it increasingly difficult to leave the studio each day and often remained longer than was necessary, wanting to spend more time learning and expanding her own thoughts. The late hour of her return to the farm resulted in her responsibilities not getting done, and that brought her parents' wrath down on her. After a scalding from Subette, she was afraid she would be prevented from returning to the studio, and diligently completed all tasks required of her without complaint, even if many were done after dusk. Jealous of the time Francesca was away, Maria became estranged.

As the weeks, then months passed, Francesca found herself regretting having to return to her home at all. Her mind was expanding, becoming creative and free, but there was no one with whom she could share her thoughts. One evening, Carlos approached and shyly asked if she would tell him what the artist discussed with her. She happily agreed, and whenever they could manage to slip away, they would meet by the cart and Carlos would sit with his chin resting on his knees, digesting her every word.

"Carlos, I shall ask the artist if you can visit his studio while I am there. You must see the musical fountain he invented. We shall have to get around Mama and Papa, but we must be determined."

Although reluctant, Signor and Signora Bellini gave permission for Carlos to occasionally visit the studio, providing he later made up any lost time on the farm. Their incentive was the promised ducats coming their way. Perhaps the artist would paint Carlos too, and that payment would increase.

While the artist worked, Carlos sat on a stool under the window and Francesca sat in her now familiar pose. The artist had given her a ribbon of embroidery which she had stitched around the low neckline of her simple gown, and a fine black veil covered her head. She wore no jewellery. The artist wanted to go against the current ornate fashion, and refused his housekeeper's offer to loan Francesca a pair of simple gold earrings. Francesca had also changed her appearance outside the studio over the months. Her hair was now smooth and she tied it up in the fashionable style she had seen wealthy ladies wearing as they paraded over the Ponte Duo. When the housekeeper gave her a worn green bedcover, she cut the fabric into squares, and stitched together a warm cloak. She liked the feel of its softness against her ankles, almost as much as the admiring glances she observed from the tradesmen when she hurried to the studio each morning.

The artist enjoyed his captive audience, and encouraged Carlos to return again and again. The trio spent many happy hours together; Carlos and Francesca were full of questions, and the artist encouraged them to express their ideas. One morning, they were surprised to see the artist dressed in elaborate garments and not the familiar stained smock. He guided them to the garden and offered refreshments. Francesca and Carlos were hesitant.

"Is there anything wrong, sire? Do you not want me to take up my pose?"

"No Francesca. You will not need to return to the studio again until I call you. The portrait is almost finished. It is time for me to work on the background."

"But, sire, surely it can't be over so quickly?" She protested.

"You are no longer needed, my child. I made a temporary arrangement with your parents and now you must return." His wrinkled features looked gaunt in the pale light. He reached out and took Francesca's hand. "Do not despair, my dear. You have brightened my life with your inquisitiveness and presence, but we came together for the sake of the portrait. It will take time to finish the background, but I will call for you to make any changes to the portrait I may find necessary. Then it will be done. You and your brother are intelligent. Continue to search within your minds."

Francesca and Carlos looked glum. Their father and mother would not encourage development of their minds. They were peasants and peasants know their place. The artist understood their dismay. "I am paying your good parents well for allowing you to sit for me, Francesca. But your payment will be a tutor to teach you and Carlos to read." His eyes twinkled as their eyes widened in disbelief. "Now, finish your refreshments and be off with you. I have important things to do."

Their bare feet skipped lightly on the rough path back to the farm, and they waved enthusiastically to the field workers gathering the first crop of turnips.

"What makes the two of you so cheerful, eh?" A tinker shouted above the rattling of assorted pots hanging from a pole balanced across his shoulders. His clothes were creased and rank, but a warm smile emerged from his grime-streaked face. Francesca and Carlos laughed but would not share their secret—not until the master had spoken to their parents.

Time seemed to stand still while the family waited for the artist to come. Francesca and Carlos lost hope. Signora Bellini, anxious to have the smooth coins in her hand, was despondent. Months passed, and then a year, and her anguish grew. "Have we been fools, Lorenzo?"

"The artist gave his word. If we are not paid, we will not starve—the land has been good to us this year."

"You are a good, patient man, my husband."

Another six months passed before the bent figure approached the hut again.

"Lorenzo, come quickly!" Subette called, excitedly, "the artist has come at last!"

Signor Bellini put down the axe. His back ached from chopping wood all morning, and he was glad to break away from such an endless task. Glad too they would now receive the long awaited compensation.

"Good day to you, Bellini. I have come to pay my debt."

"You are welcome, sire."

The humble man stepped back to allow the artist entrance to the dusty room. Signora Bellini took the leather pouch from the artist's outstretched hand, and closed her fingers over the heavy coins. "Grazie mille, sire."

"You have your payment, Signora, but I have further words for you and your husband." The children gathered around the doorway, jostling for a prized position to hear the conversation within. "Let us discuss arrangements I have made concerning Francesca and your son Carlos." The artist chose his words carefully. "Doors are beginning to open in education, not only for children of princes, but impoverished children as well." He emphasized the importance now placed on reading, and pleaded for Carlos' chance. He paid special care in his plea for Francesca. "Women are now being educated, but they are not encouraged to go beyond good manners and how to raise their children. Francesca is unique and I am determined her mind will not be wasted."

Their father's voice sounded stern when he called Francesca and Carlos to him. Silently, they edged forward. The other children crowded closer, hoping the two were going to be punished. After all,

106

had not Francesca and Carlos escaped from their responsibilities, and put on airs thinking themselves better than the rest of them?

"The artist desires to arrange for a tutor to teach you both to read." Signor Bellini announced. "Your mother and I have agreed, but we are troubled this arrangement will interfere with the management of our land. Therefore, lessons will take place only upon you completing your duties. They are to come first."

"Si, Papa." Francisco and Carlos could not keep the excitement from their voices. They were relieved their parents had given in so easily.

"The artist is giving you a chance we never hoped for. As you both learn, you will teach your brothers and sisters." Lorenzo turned to his wife and took her rough hands in his. "Your mother and I know only how to till the land. Who would have thought our children would learn to read? How proud we will be." Lorenzo's voice filled with emotion. "We are grateful, sire."

The other children were restrained by nervousness. Book learning held little appeal. They were content to work on the farm. If Francesca and Carlos wanted more, so be it. Francesca moved closer to the artist.

"You taught us the world is not restricted to this small plot of earth. Through reading we will know no boundaries." She leaned forward and kissed his cheek. "Thank you, sire. You are giving us a priceless gift, indeed. We will not to let you down."

The artist blushed. He admonished himself for such an irritating weakness that was known to his colleagues but continued to cause him much embarrassment. "I have no fear of that, my dear. I do want you to understand, however, that for you and your sisters, it will be more difficult to reach for knowledge. To be informed is not a requirement of a woman. Your intelligence may be a cause for concern to others, perhaps making them feel inadequate, but I trust you will never give in."

"I assure you, I will not."

The artist turned to the happy throng. "The portrait of Signorina Francesca Bellini is far from complete; however, I invite you all to my studio for a private viewing of what has been accomplished thus far."

"Subette, we shall see it at last."

"Yes, Lorenzo. At last."

The artist welcomed them warmly to his studio at the Ponte Due, and offered refreshments, the like of which the family had never seen or tasted before. Each dish was elegantly served. Venison was thinly sliced, and tender cocks' combs were marinated in a sauce so rich and delicious, the housekeeper brought them a second pot. The younger children, knowing only the blemished fruit gathered from their own trees, took full advantage of the large juicy figs, golden peaches and red cherries overflowing the tureen. Being sensitive to their lack of exposure to such things before, the artist took care to show only a selected few of his paintings to the ignorant family. He explained simply the intent of each picture and made certain not to overwhelm them. When it came time to unveil the long awaited portrait, he realized how fond he had become of them all. Excitedly, they crowded around the easel.

"Remember the picture is far from finished. I still have much work to do until I am satisfied."

As the artist removed the cloth, they gasped in unison. The gentle, subtle beauty of the image was unpretentious. Looking out was a Francesca unknown to them. She was seated with both her hands resting easily on the arm of a chair. The artist had magically transformed her tanned and roughened skin to a warm satin, and hair escaping from a gossamer veil was tamed. Below a high forehead, her eyes seemed to follow each of them as they moved around the picture. The left side of her mouth turned up slightly, adding both pensiveness and sweetness to her expression. The onlookers were moved to tears.

"Francesca, you are beautiful." Marie slipped her arm through her sister's and they drew close.

"It is a masterpiece, sire." Signor Bellini's face creased into a wide grin. "I have no words."

The artist was touched by the family's response, and he could not have wished for a more positive reception of his work. He had used a new method of adding a glaze with the pigment instead of using egg yolk, and this had resulted in a soft lustre to the colours. He had even experimented with two perspectives that produced an air of mystery. The family knew nothing about such techniques, but they appreciated his achievement, and were thrilled to see their beloved countryside depicted in the background. He had included the very path they took to reach the market and the nearby seven arched Ponte Buriano. The portrait was a long way from finished, but he knew the final work would be a stunning success. Now sixty-five years of age, he had accomplished many great works, but this piece had become his passion. Under no circumstances would Francesca be named, even to his benefactor who had commissioned the work. He decided on the title *Lady Lisa* in order to increase speculation and gossip about who she was. Satisfied, he smiled to himself, knowing the puzzle would cause continued discussion long after his death.

The mule struggled for secure footing under the weight of the overcrowded cart. The refreshing nip in the air was welcomed after the heat of a scorching day. Like a whisper, an owl flew passed, its cry piercing the darkness. Signora Bellini sang a familiar folk song, and the younger children joined in the chorus. Their voices carried across the fields, and disappeared into the mist-shrouded distance. Eventually, the youngsters fell asleep in the arms of their older siblings; the rest of the family lapsed into silence, reflecting on the day's remarkable events. How changed their lives had become because of their encounter with the generous stranger. Although the artist told them he was well known throughout Italy, his name was meaningless to them. Signor Bellini guided the mule over the rutted path towards the barn. Francesca leaned over her father's shoulder and rested her cheek against his. Signor Bellini kissed the top of her head. "I'm proud of you, daughter. We've had an astonishing episode in our lives."

"It will be a relief to get back to normal, Lorenzo," Signora Bellini yawned. "We will keep this secret for all time. Our neighbours have no interest."

Signor Bellini pulled the mule to a halt and stepped down from the cart. "Wake up children, we're home. Maria, help Mama with the bambini. And you, *Mona Lisa*, help me put the mule away."

"Yes, Papa," Francesca laughed and led the weary mule into the bar.

THE BUTTON

I'd been walking for about a couple of miles—the ocean was in a calm mood, and gently lapped against the shore, leaving a delicate lace of foam. At that early hour the sand was already agitated by legions of footprints. Surfers waited patiently for the wave that would provide the addictive thrill. They were like pods of porpoise; their wetsuits dissolving any individuality. Groups of grey and white plovers raced to the water's edge. Orange bills at the ready, they speared tasty morsels with precise timing and then, reversing gears, sped to avoid a dousing. Ignored, I walked on and picked up a fan shaped shell to add to the assortment in the coffee tin I carried. I had enough to cover a picture frame I intended as a gift for a friend. I turned and started back, walking slowly, resisting. The sand was beginning to absorb heat from the sun, and I puckered my toes against it. Lengths of dried seaweed and odd shapes of driftwood added to the litter scattered by unthinking intruders—plastic bottles, pieces of balloons—even a sandal. I collected as I walked on and quickly my arms were full. Frustrated, I dumped the junk into a trash bin.

"Awful, isn't it?" I looked over. A young man was waxing a surfboard.

"It really is!" Something caught my eye. I bent to pick it up.

"What you got there?"

"It's a button—a brass button." I held it out and he came over.

I rubbed the sand off, and exposed the embossed shape of a five-petal flower. The sand had worked the metal so it was polished and bright.

"Never seen anything like that before. Out of place here."
I nodded and slipped the button into my pocket.

Upon arriving at my home, I took the tin of shells out to the patio to rinse any sandy residue off with the hose. Placed together on the table, they looked pale, anaemic, but the spray brought out a palette of orange, blues, browns and cream; brilliance usually revealed to only those who patrol beneath the waves. Quickly, the heat of the sun returned the colours to subtle opaque again. It was peaceful in the garden, and I lost myself in the pleasure of coating a picture frame with porcelain-like fans, no less delicate than those fluttered by graceful Geishas.

Pleased with my finished creation, I wandered into the bathroom to clean up. My pockets were sticky with sand and I stripped carefully. I'd learned sweeping up those tiny granules was a thankless job, and was still challenged to get rid of those that had spilled a while ago and seemed to have procreated in the corners of the baseboard. I took the brass button from my pant pocket, and placed it in the soap dish.

It was a few days later before I took up the button again. It had been so out of place on the sand. Did it wash up from a land far, far away—carried on undulating swells of heavy curves racing toward a final destination, or was it simply tossed away by a beachcomber because the trashcan was inconveniently out of reach? I pressed my thumb against the embossed flower and absently put it back into the soap dish where it remained for several weeks, building up a coating of soap deposits and tarnish. I got so used to it being there, I didn't notice it any more. It was weeks later before we got reacquainted. Friends were coming over and the house got a thorough cleaning to save my reputation. I scrubbed the hardened crust of soap and was pleased to see the brass polished up quite nicely. The back of the button showed small chips and an indentation as if its journey to the California shore had been a rough one. It was only about an inch across and devoid of any official mark. Where had it come from?

Whose hand had crafted its manufacture? I took it into my office and placed it on my desk. Friends would soon be arriving and demanding food.

I had a number of letters to write and decided on a damp spring morning to show some discipline and tackle at least a couple. Once I got going, it was easy to lose myself in internal dialogue through written words. I felt close to my father so many miles away in England as I told him about new seeds I'd planted in the garden, how the Southern California sandy soil took a lot of replenishing to bring about my desired display of colour and variety, and what plants I had chosen to encourage birds and friendly insects. I complained about the hardship of getting lupine seeds to germinate in the coastal climate. His garden was a mass of tall purple and pink spikes, coming up year after year without any codling. My obedience to friendly suggestions had resulted in plants making it to two to three inches tall; then, for some mysterious reason, shrivelled and gave up. I told him *I* was not about to give up, however, and already had seeds soaking for thirty-six hours, per a local nurseryman's advice, in an effort to encourage an improved result. I signed my name at the bottom of the page and felt acutely aware of the miles separating us. I addressed the envelope and, as it was my practice to display my bragger individuality, placed a thick blob of warm black wax on the back flap. It was then that the button caught my eye and, almost absently, I picked it up and pressed it into the soft wax. The imprint of the flower was perfect, and complimented the subject of my screed to my father. I happily mailed the letter later that day.

I continued to use the button when sealing personal correspondence, and even had a block made so I could add it to my signature or stamp a piece of stationery. That little flower became my trademark. It became so well known to family and friends that it was unnecessary for my name to appear in order to be identified. In a burst of creative energy, I copied the design and made brooches from tiny smooth cockleshells gathered from the sands at low tide. I glued five individual pieces in place onto a metal clip, and then added a coat of varnish to bring out the colours of calcium build up. Nature had produced a subtle work of art, and it was satisfying to see friends wearing these little badges of alliance.

It was probably about a year later when I had lunch with a couple of British friends. We were to discuss the possibility of becoming U.S. citizens. They had brought along a middle-aged Asian woman who was giving consideration to the same idea. May Kuboto was Japanese, and had been living in California with her family for twenty years. Her short straight hair was tinged with silver, but her skin was as smooth. She must have been in her sixties, and perhaps because of the fat-rich diet of this wealthy society, was as rounded as a melon. She had a gentleness and grace about her, and I found myself immediately drawn to her. At the end of two very pleasant hours, we stood outside the restaurant to say our goodbyes. May hesitated for a moment, and then pointed to the shell pins we were wearing, and asked about their significance. I explained about finding the brass button and its influence in the pin creation, and resolved to give her one next time we got together.

May came to tea a couple of weeks later, and it was fun to discuss the differences and similarities of our particular cultures when it came to tea ceremonies. I'd set up a tray complete with a fine starched cotton cloth, my porcelain china, a selection of finger sandwiches and petit fours, and placed it on a small table in front of where I would sit. My teapot was large, and covered in a quilted "cosy" to keep the contents hot. My cups were large. Even the plates seemed large, although they were the smallest of the set. As May draped a napkin across her lap and helped herself to a sandwich, I could see the difficulty she was having in balancing a cup of hot tea on a saucer in one hand and a plate on her knee. As May explained, the Japanese serve their tea in very small cups from very small pots, and are usually seated in front of a low table on which to place the china. There is no milk or sugar involved as with the British brew—just refreshing understated flavourful tea. The British ritual seems awkward in comparison and certainly requires skills I hadn't contemplated before. Perhaps our larger Western legs provided a wider surface for plate balancing as we sipped. May and I were soon laughing at such antics and quickly moved ourselves to a more comfortable spot at the dining table. May proudly explained that in Japan, the tea ceremony is a traditional ritual influenced by Zen Buddhism; water represents *yin* and the fire used to heat the water is *yang*. Even modern Japanese practice Tea as an important social event from which they feel a sense of national belonging. Harmony is sought with the environment and all others through concentration on beautiful rituals, self-discipline and personal discovery. Sharing a cup of tea with family and friends was an immensely important and pleasurable time out for both of us, a respite if you will. May's voice was soft and wistful, and I became aware of my own intense homesickness.

It was on May's third visit when I gave her a shell pin, welcoming her to our small fraternity. Her almond shaped eyes glistened with pleasure. On impulse, I got the brass button from my office to show her the impetus behind the pin's design. She took the button and gazed at it in silence for a moment or two.

"It's Japanese," she said. I was dumbfounded.

"I've wondered where it came from. I found it on the beach over a year ago."

"It's a naval uniform button."

"Are you sure? You can tell just like that?"

"My father was an officer in the Japanese Imperial Navy. He was killed in 1943, so I don't remember him, but my mother kept his dress uniform on display. Buttons like this one were on the jacket. As a little girl, I would help my mother polish them. I think she held on to the hope if she kept the uniform impeccable, it would somehow bring him back. It took years for her to admit he would not return."

"Those were terrible years for so many." I put my hand on May's arm. "I'm glad we're friends."

115

May squeezed my hand. "Yes, me too."

I sat for a long time after May left. I absently rubbed the button against my thumb and thought of the journey this small fastener had taken. Had it been on the uniform of a proud officer killed in action, or just fallen from a slack thread due to slovenliness? How many storms and currents had it taken to land it on Sunset Beach, California? How had it avoided being swallowed by a hungry deep-water shadow? Or had it? Questions and more questions. I found myself smiling. This small, insignificant object had come thousands of perilous miles over a period of many decades, to eventually rest in the hand of a British immigrant walking along a Californian beach on a spring morning. It seemed ironic that a floral motif—seemingly so without malice, so mundane—identified an enemy naval officer and now, so many years later, had become my logo of recognition. I thought of all who had fought in a war where butchery took place beside heroics; draped in khaki, navy or air corps blue, sons and daughters, husbands and wives marched into a hell while the band played on. Well, this small object had brought about a friendship that transcended all of that. On my next visit to May's immaculate and peaceful apartment, I gave her the button in a small dark blue leather box. After all, it belonged to her. We are United States citizens now, but May has a special kinship because these California shores gave her father back to her—through a small, sand-polished brass button.

THE GAME

"Miiind ouutt!"

"What?"

"Mind out, I'm going to hit the ball."

"You don't yell *mind out*. You call *Fore*."

"Four? How utterly ridiculous. Four what?"

"Not four. Fore."

"That's what I said—four."

"Babe, listen. Fore!"

"Spell it, Tommy."

"F o r e. Fore. It's the warning to other golfers who may be in range of your ball."

"Oh! All right, now out of the way. I'm going to hit off. Which stick shall I use?"

"What do you mean *stick*? Club—which *club*! And its *tee* off! I know you English have your own way of saying things but you'd think you'd know the correct terms—the game came from your country, after all!"

"It came from Scotland, Tom—not England. Anyway, I really don't know why you're making such a fuss. It's only the two of us playing. You may be an American but you surely know what I mean."

"That's not the point. You have to learn the terms and etiquette of golf. It is a very serious game. Please pay attention."

"I'm trying!"

"Yes, you are, very trying!"

"Now, now. Don't get mean. Well, here goes. Fore!"

"Not bad. A lot of divots to gain those two yards. In case you don't know, divots are all those chips you've cut out of the green with that *stick*. Also, for your information, you did a worm burner which means you struck a shot that barely got off the ground and the ball just rolled."

"A worm burner? You can't be serious? Who on earth came up with that nonsense? You seem to forget I'm just a beginner. We'd better let the group behind us go ahead. GO AHEAD. DON'T WANT TO HOLD YOU UP."

"Why did you do that?"

"What's wrong now?"

"If you let players ahead of us, we'll never get off the first tee. It's embarrassing."

"I don't want them breathing down my neck. You're doing a good job of that. It's obviously a mistake I came out."

"Please don't sulk. I can't stand sulking."

"You can't stand me, you mean."

"That is not what I said. Don't start getting teary-eyed; just take the club and a fresh ball and tee off again. You may do better."

"Why don't you go first and I'll follow you?"

"No, you go. Here's the driver. Try again. See that flag? That's where you aim."

"It's an awfully long way, isn't it? Oh, well—here goes."

"That is much better, probably all of *ten* yards! Well done."

"I think so, and a lot less divots. I may have a knack for this game, after all. Okay, your turn."

"Don't get carried away, sweetheart. Look—notice how I'm standing? Knees bent slightly. Rear out a little. I keep my eye on the shoulder of the ball at all times."

"You look as if you're about to sit on a potty. Not very dignified, you know."

"You're getting on my nerves."

"Sorry!"

"See that? Did you pay attention to my stroke? That's probably 150 yards. With practice you will be doing the same thing."

"How much practice?"

"If you go on a course two-three times a week, I'd say probably a couple of years."

"I could be dead before then. You're kidding, right?"

"Yes, I'm kidding, but if you want to play well, it takes a lot of time and effort. You do what it takes."

"Can't I play just for fun?"

"Not with me. I want to be challenged by my partner."

"Will this be a condition of our marriage?"

"Oh, come on! You're being silly. I love you and want us to enjoy being out on the course together. With a few lessons, you will soon catch on. Now, pay attention and take your time. Balance the distribution of weight throughout the swing. Look ahead before you make contact with the ball—think things through, honey. Keep your left arm straight as you make the swing. No-no! Not like that! Position your wrists at the top of the backswing so the top wrist is bent slightly inward."

"Fore!"

"Good grief, you chunked it!"

"Meaning?"

"You made contact behind the ball, and your club dug into the ground too deeply. Just look at that groove in the green."

"I'm doing my best, Tom. No need to get your knickers in a twist."

"You know, Beth, the British terms you use are completely wacky and not at all amusing. I'm going to walk down to my ball. I'll wait for you there."

"I'm freezing!"

"You did say to take my time. I'm really chuffed it only took eight hits to get here."

"Strokes, honey. *Strokes*! Not *hits*."

"I think this game is going to give me a stroke!"

"And you'll give me one if you don't stop chattering and pay attention to what you're doing."

"Really, darling, such a kerfuffle! You're getting carried away a bit don't you think?"

"PLEASE! JUST HIT THE BALL. DON'T say anything more."

"There is certainly no need to shout at me. I don't know what's gotten into you."

"What was supposed to be a pleasant afternoon together has become an *un*pleasant squabble! I understand you've had little experience of the game; you made that clear, but you're behaving like an irrational child."

"How dare you speak to me like that? You're too serious, Tommy. You need to lighten up. I don't think you've smiled or shown any humour since we've been out."

"Golf is not a joke. It's a difficult sport; even the pros have difficult days. There's a lot of passion involved. It's only natural offensive personality traits come through from everyone playing, but you learn to ignore them. It's all part of the game. It's a good thing we came out today—it's revealed we have a major problem. I love the game; love being out in the environment, but it's caused contention between us after a couple of hours. I'm not sure how to handle it."

"Yes, we have a problem all right—everything has gone to pot. I've met the true Tom Casey. AND I DON'T LIKE IT!"

"Oh, really? You are a bright woman, but your behaviour today makes me question what's gotten into you. Golf requires skill and wisdom at every level. You may not have the skills yet, but you could with effort. You are not even trying. It seems just a…what is the idiom you English say…a lark?"

"Are you saying I'm stupid? Huh? It takes one to know one! Marriage to a pompous ass like you would be impossible. These few hours have been a blessing in disguise; now we both know the true personality of the other."

"Don't pull the tearful act on me, Beth Ross. You're right— marriage would be a mistake, as today had clearly shown!"

"I'm leaving—out of my way. I never want to see you again. I'm taking the trolley. *You* can walk!"

"It's a CART! Who in their right mind would call it a trolley, for crying out loud! Can't you get anything straight in that block of nothing you call a mind?"

"What are you screaming about? You're making a scene in front of people."

"What people? There's no one around. They've all left because they can't play when it's dark! Here, take the damn key to the *trolley*, and take your bundle of *sticks, and your ball.* Or do you have your own name for that too?"

"I have a few names for *you*! I'm getting as far away from you as possible. Oh, damn! Look what you've made me do!"

"*I* made you hit your head on the safety-bar? Good Lord! You're a disaster."

"Never mind about asking if I'm all right or anything. Typical male."

"Easy does it. There's blood on your cheek. Let me look."

"It's your fault—you keep arguing. I can't think straight. Ouch! That hurts. But only a little; you *can* be gentle when you want to."

"I want to, because I love you. Golf is a game I happen to love too, but I love you much more. Now, will you be sensible and get into the cart so I can take you home? The movie starts at 8:30. By the time we freshen up, we shall hardly have time to eat."

"You love me really, Tommy?"

"Yes-yes! 'Course I do!"

"Can I have one last hit before we go? I'll be quick."

"What's the point—you won't be able to see the ball now the course lights are off. You're a long way from the hole."

"You could stand by the hole to be my marker. Please, Tom."

"It's pointless, honey, but all right. Anything for a quiet life."

"I'm glad you are wearing that white sweater. I can see it quite well."

"Okay, I'm here. Now remember what I said."

"Here goes. I'll try not to hit you."

"Try *really* hard! Make sure your axis remains in a constant position throughout the swing, honey. Good god! I must be dreaming, Beth. You aced it. I never thought I'd say such a thing to you! Well done, darling. Stay where you are. I'll come to you."

"I need a hug, Tom. Try not to hate me—I've a confession. I caddied for my father at St. Andrew's when I was in my early teens in exchange for lessons. I've been playing ever since, and—so I'm told, I'm pretty good."

"You set me up? Why, in heaven's name? What have the last few hours been about? If you are such a good player why have you played the fool? I don't get it."

"I wanted to check *you* out, Tom. I wanted to see how seriously you took the game. You see, my dear, your love of the game is a condition of marriage for *me*! We were indisputably smitten with each other, but what can you learn about a person in a couple of months? It was my father's suggestion that we go out to the course together—he must have seen things that I have just discovered about you. You're serious about golf all right but you have no charity. I do play very well and we could, indeed, enjoy the course together, but calling me names and barking directions have made me aware our lives together could be much the same."

"Well, Beth Ross, your father and you certainly had the last laugh. You played me, and I fell for it. Naturally, he wants someone a lot better for you but it is not his decision if we stay together or walk away. That is up to you and me."

"It was unfair of us, but better to find out now than later if we're compatible. He loves me, even above golf. He wants me to be happy, Tom. You and I want that too, right?"

"Of course, and we've both learned things during this escapade. You now know I love golf, and take it very seriously. I now know you do too. Your father's ploy has not changed how I feel about you. Yes, you got my goat all right. I got pretty mean, and have no excuse. If we stayed together, I would most likely behave abominably again whenever we set foot on a course, but that monster would not drive home with us. I'm generally pretty docile in the life beyond."

"I'm feeling badly now. You were such a cad this afternoon, but it *was* a pretty horrid thing to do to you."

"Can I kiss you?"

"Yes, please do."

"Do you still love me? Just a tiny bit?"

"Yes, Tommy. I'm afraid I do—deeply."

"Are you thinking what I'm thinking?"

"I hope so."

"Then let's go home and prove it. I'm sure we can find our way in the dark if we hold on tightly to each other"

THE SCRUFF

There is a small stray cat that roams our street block like a homeless waif who looks upon the world with eyes that challenge, dare. I'm convinced he is a male because there is no way a feminine gene could exist within that feisty moth-eaten character. He wanders the gutters that are often full of dried leaves and water runoff, and spends lazy hours basking in the sun, head propped up against the curb, eyes not quite closed, so a thin line of Citrine yellow affirms he is in control. I know people who place themselves in a similar position but spread out on a chaise lounge. When I take my daily walks, he stares across the road at me, but makes no move. Those yellow eyes are emotionless—as if cataracts of dust cover them, distorting his view of the world by extracting any interest in life beyond his chosen territory. He reminds me of a shapeless rag rug, the kind made from patches of material taken from old clothing. My grandmother made one from my brother's grey school uniform trousers and it was placed inside her front door to wipe our feet on before continuing down the hall. It was anything but pretentious but served its purpose extremely well for years. This cat is remarkably similar—a well-used patchwork of black and grey; the colours now faded by dirt and burrs.

Although tangles and fur clumps prevent a full stride, he ambles along very well, increasing the lackadaisical saunter to an impressive pace when necessary. My neighbour directly across from me feeds the strays from the area twice a day, and this errant spirit meanders to her front porch with a swagger that is impressive enough to ensure other hungry drifters take second seating. The menu is unchanging: Friskies, on time and plentiful. At sunup a damp shadow slinks along the side of the road. Is it too hungry—could it be too stubborn—to avoid a dousing from the early morning sprinklers in order to eat first? As daylight increases, the shadow turns out to be the street-tough. He emerges from the neighbour's porch to survey those subservient felines waiting patiently for their own breakfast; they know their place. He takes his time, as if acknowledging his power to prolong their hunger pangs. Once his own appetite is satiated, he parks himself on the raised doorstep. Leisurely licking his paws, he acts out a charade of grooming and, with a coated tongue, cleans off a last crumb from those tight, thin lips. His ablutions completed, he nonchalantly strolls away, looking back once, as if to say, okay boys, go and get it. At six-thirty precisely in the evening, he returns for dinner, and the whole show starts over again. Did TS Eliot have such a character in mind for his book of poems *Old Possums Book of Practical Cats?* But then, Old Deuteronomy was too much a gentleman and well-groomed in Andrew Lloyd Webber's adaptation for his Broadway show, *CATS*.

I was taking the trashcans in from the curb a couple of days ago. Dusk was just settling in, and the remaining light was fading like a soft breath. Wafts of star jasmine perfume filled the cooling air. Kitchen windows of the single story stuccos glowed invitingly as evening meals were being prepared. In the middle of the road sat our boy intently cleaning himself. It was an extraordinary sight and I wished I had a camera handy—a photograph would be proof I wasn't hallucinating. He looked worse than usual. He must have rolled in grass cuttings for green spikes were sticking out all over him like bobby pins trying to tame a wacky hairstyle. With one leg straight up against his shoulder, he was attending to his belly. Upon seeing me, he paused with an icy stare. *Got something on your mind?* Through telepathy I replied, *I'm not getting into it with you,* and turned my back.

Later, when I took my dog for her evening stroll, a passing car swerved, its headlamp beaming over the body of a small animal lying flat on the asphalt of the road. There was no movement. My breath caught in my throat. The beastie had been run over! Commanding my dog to stay on the pavement, I went over to the motionless bundle and bent down, slowly putting my hand out and calling softly. No response. I stepped closer. Two menacing amber bolts of light stared back at me and abruptly the head lifted. The unexpected movement startled me, causing me to lose my balance and I fell over on my side. The asphalt was still warm from the day's heat, and I realized this was what that rogue was taking advantage of. He slowly got up, and came to stand over my face. Head down, he snarled, baring his teeth. The fetid stink of cesspit living rose up. I watched as he turned and unhurriedly walked across to the other side of the street. We have a Neighbourhood Watch for such a person but what can you do about a cat—this cat? Our cat? I can't think of a single thing.

WILDERNESS AT RISK

The sails of giant grey ears fanned back and forth, their veins extended to full capacity. The open cracks in the elephant cow's hide held no moisture, but were blanketed over in scabs of black flies. The sun was merciless. Impalas stood silently, their white and tanned heads down in an exhausted attempt to fight the heat. There were no shade trees, no scrub to chew upon for moisture and strength; nothing but the relentlessness of blistering air. A young wildebeest staggered in the last throws before death. Its ribs starkly evident beneath an insect infested hide. Jonathan held the camera steady but found it impossible to impassively watch the horror that played out before him.

He had experienced the semi-arid lands of the Serengeti for the first time as a tourist several years previously. The crater's unique fragile beauty became a part of him, and he was acutely affected by the problems facing the very survival of the Great Rift Valley region. He had returned to the United States and earned a master's degree as a wildlife conservationist. With financial backing from the World Wildlife Society, he volunteered to return a year ago to take up the lancet against the practice by the Maasai people of grazing their cattle on the same locale terrain that could not sustain continued over grazing. The Maasai's wealth was in their livestock, and each beast was treated with respect. A proud people, they did not welcome outsiders telling them they must change their long held tradition; however, they were heading for serious problems.

Jonathan knew he faced enormous opposition, but he had gathered materials for a presentation to show the depth of the problem. The photographs were an important part of his strategy to promote his cause. When he met with Murunga, the headman of the local Maasai village later that afternoon, he was eyed suspiciously. He was not able to speak the Maasai's language of Maa, but was fluent in Swahili which the tribe understood. Mulumba invited Jonathan to sit on the dusty ground in front of him, and presented a bowl of liquid. Jonathan accepted the bowl and drank the concoction of milk and blood in quick, noisy gulps. He was watched carefully by the small group of elders who had joined them.

"Murunga, have you thought over what we discussed on my last visit? By rotating the grazing areas, the cattle will prosper as your people will. If the cattle are transported to the areas indicated on this map during the spring and summer seasons, the grasses will not be over-grazed and will recover. The animals will return to your village for the winter as usual, and be sustained with fodder that has been gathered locally and stored." Jonathan pointed to the route on the map spread between them, and brought out the Polaroid camera. "Look at these photographs I took this morning. There are going to be no winners, my friend, unless we work together on a solution to avoid such devastation. By rotating grazing regions, the earth has a chance to heal. Scrub, trees and grasses will bloom again after the rains, and their seeds will bring back the richness and beauty of this land. My suggestion is not the whole answer, but it is a beginning."

"You call me friend yet you want to change my peoples' lives to suit you. I see for myself animals are dying. Your pictures are not needed. During my lifetime, I have known when there was no break in the sweep of wildebeest on the horizon. The elephant, zebra, and antelope thrived and lived in peace. Now, if the elephant eats first, the acacia tree is destroyed and there is no shade. The grass is scorched and dies, leaving nothing for the zebra and antelope. Perhaps it is God's will that the wild ones should perish to leave grasses for my people?"

Jonathan knew he had a cunning adversary, but he was a patient man and there was much to gain. He acknowledged Murunga's fierce personal pride in his strength and physical charisma, as evidenced by his intricate hair style that involved many narrow braids tied behind his head and covered in red ochre and fat that gave of a pungent animal odour. He was to be reckoned with in spite of his many years. Murunga's wrinkled brow deepened as he studied the landscape that he had depended on all his life.

"A few weeks after my circumcision, I proved my bravery as a young worrier by killing an equally brave lion. According to tradition, I stalked the massive male for five days, ending the game with several mortal lances from my spirited spear. I won the admiration of my family and village when I returned blooded from the hunt, and wearing the lion's magnificent black mane. Now there are so few lions left, the young men are forbidden to hunt them, and they will never know the intense satisfaction I myself have known."

"Murunga, if you persuade the elders that this plan will benefit your village, the wild animals could stand a chance too, and that is what I am asking for—a chance." Murunga recognized the sincerity in Jonathan's tone, and knew although they came from different worlds, they were united in their love for the Serengeti.

"I will give the idea more consideration. Return tomorrow for my answer."

Jonathan watched the villagers with admiration. They were a nation of beautiful people with an average height of over six feet with thin straight limbs. He contemplated the dependence they had on their cattle; huge beasts with soft brown eyes. Seldom were they slaughtered, for their number made a man wealthy. The main diet for the people consisted of a little meat, and cattle blood mixed with milk. An animal's jugular vein was speared and the blood collected in a container to be topped off with cow milk. The wound was then plugged with mud, and the animal showed no ill affect. Jonathon observed the small group of elders dressed in many strings of beads and red and purple cloth walk away from him. He knew he needed patience for there was much to learn from their simplicity yet fearsome pride. Light was beginning to fade. The village was a circle of huts made of cow dung that allowed for coolness in summer and warmth in winter. The precious cattle and goats were kept within the circle during the night as protection against thieves and predators. The constant cloud of hungry flies seemed only a minor irritation to endure, and little attention was paid to their investigation of nostrils and eyes. The sun slipped beyond the edge of the horizon, leaving a silhouette of stunted trees in its fiery aura.

The sun was without mercy when Jonathan stood in front of Murunga again. "The elders have talked together and we have our answer. We will try it your way for one of each season. If there is no change for the better, we will revert to our customs of today. If there is improvement, we will talk again at that time."

"This is all I am asking. Thank you, Murunga, and thank you to your gracious people." The small group enthusiastically shook hands and grinned. "Now we can begin." Jonathan said.

The Maasai villagers kept their word. As each season arrived, the young boys took the cattle to prearranged areas to graze. Jonathan was in a constant state of anxiety. The rains were lighter than usual during the wet season, but with the cattle settled in an upper plain, the grasses were not sheered to total destruction by their insatiable appetites. Sweet new grasses were given time to mature to a lush depth. Wild herds benefited too, and there was contentment and docility over the land. During birthing, the grasses and young bushes were stable and gave protection to the new life.

Jonathan continued to worry, afraid to believe the plan had worked so perfectly. As the passing months numbered twelve, only then did he begin to relax and take personal pride in the success of the operation. There was joyful satisfaction for everyone as they viewed the developing splendour now surrounded them. Although wildlife had not increased dramatically, the numbers seemed secure, and hunting was ample. The herds of cattle were healthier from the long trek to the grazing grounds, benefiting from exercise and nutritious grasses. It was difficult for Murunga and Jonathan not to feel complacent over the success of their alliance.

Josh, a senior field officer, rushed into the office. "Come quickly, Jonathan…about two miles north. We've got big trouble."

Jonathan drove his Land Rover recklessly, following too closely to the vehicle in front so that the road's dry surface churned up by the racing wheels filled his parched throat. He arrived covered in sweat and dust. A half dozen or so uniformed guards were waiting for him, talking quietly among themselves. "Over there." One pointed to a small clump of bushes, hardly large enough to hide the carnage scattered between. "They had machine guns. Must have just opened fire on the whole herd. Even the new calves have been killed." The guide shook his head in disgust. Jonathan and Josh walked among the butchered bodies of ten elephants. Their tusks were gone, leaving hideous cavities and gaping bloody wounds. Already the carcasses were ballooning and the stench was strong. Overhead buzzards circled and jackals and hyenas quickened their pace in hast to join in the looming feast. The two men stood silently, unable to speak through anger and sorrow at the scene of horror.

Jonathan pulled himself together as best he could, and gave the order to return to camp. There was nothing they could do. The carcasses would be put to good use by the scavengers.

"We seem to solve one difficult problem and then another comes along that's even more challenging. This may be my first encounter with poachers, but I'll take them on with everything I've got." He turned to Josh. "I want all hands to be at headquarters by first light, but you and I have some thinking to do on this now. Let's go."

"I'll put the word out, Jonathan." Josh gave orders quietly to the guards, and followed Jonathan.

Jonathan did not sleep that night. He could not get the image of the savage slaughter from his mind. When the patrol arrived for the meeting, he was ready.

"We are going to have to patrol the areas circled here and here." He pointed to several markings on a map pinned to the wall. "We will have three armed men to each team, and they will go out at different times. The schedule must change constantly to keep those bastards on their toes. If they think we keep to a timetable, we'll never catch them."

"Jonathan, you have a visitor."

Jonathan turned to see Murunga in a robe of red and wearing several rows of coloured beads. His ears lobes were stretched under the weight of heavy beaded hoops. The four elders accompanying him were equally magnificent.

"Murunga, this is a surprise. What can I do for you?" Jonathan shook Murunga's hand, but was impatient. He wanted to get on with the task at hand.

"My friend, we have heard of the slaughter of the elephants and my villagers want to help. We have many young warriors who cannot hunt for sport for fear of the law so let them hunt with the law's blessing."

"Murunga, you are an answer to a prayer. We are going over the patrols now, and could do with as many men as you can spare. We have another great fight on our hands, old friend, and I am glad to have you at my side again. All the hard work we put into rehabilitating areas of this great valley was a success. Together, we can work to see this butchery is stopped."

"You must understanding, Jonathan. These poachers are very poor and this is a way to make money for their villages so there is food to eat."

"No! These men are not poor, Murunga. They use guns to kill elephants and rhinoceroses and sell their tusks and horns to foreigners for huge profits. They have no interest in the meat to feed their hungry villagers; they leave it behind to rot. It is senseless killing and I am going to do all I can to put an end to it."

"Then I am with you. Tell me what my people can do and we will succeed."

"I will give everything I have to see that we do." Jonathan gestured to the guards around him. "My men are committed too, but we must not be naive. We are few and are entering a war zone with an armed enemy. It will be very dangerous, but we will be protecting some of the world's most important species from poaching, illegal trade and habitat loss. We are not alone. There are many organizations working all over Africa to achieve the same goal, but this is our territory, and we will fight with everything we have to win."

"Do not worry, Jonathan. Much is achieved by few. We know the Serengeti well, and will be a strong adversary." Murunga said firmly.

"We will succeed because it is the right thing to do." Jonathan went to the door, and opened it wide. "Let's begin."

And…for fun…

———— ∞ ————

BE CAREFUL WHAT YOU ASK FOR

It is dark on the narrow road. The car windshield wipers cannot keep up with the torrential rain. Fay looks over at her husband. "Please slow down, Roger. You know how scared I get in the rain. You're going much too fast."

"Do you want to drive?" He smirks.

"Of course not, but do slow down, please! We've got children at home. This is dangerous."

"You're such a nag, Fay. Always complaining about something. Either shut up or I'll pull over and you can get out."

"Don't be silly, Roger. I don't know why you always race along when you know how it upsets me."

The rain drops beat like a drum on the car roof and the windows fog up. Roger tries wiping the windshield with his hand but it immediately fogs up again. Angrily, he puts his foot down on the accelerator, and the car roars ahead.

"Why are you so cruel? Stop the car right now! I'm not going to end up a paraplegic because of your madness! Let me out."

The car skids to an unsteady stop at a rest area. Roger leans over and opens the passenger door. "Happy now?"

"What are you doing?"

"Waiting for you to get out. Be quick about it, the rain is coming inside."

"You're not serious. Come on, Roger. I just want you to slow down a little. That's not too much to ask for, surely."

A man in rain gear comes up to the car. "Do you need any help? I'm parked back there with the tow truck."

"No-no, everything is fine. My wife insists on getting out, although I haven't a clue what she thinks she's going to do." He leans over Fay. "Out you get, then." He pushes her out of the passenger seat, and quickly closes the door. The car roars as he drives off.

"I hate you, Roger!" She shouts against the increasing wind. "As soon as I get home, I'm getting a divorce." She sobs, realizing what she has got herself into. She begins to walk along the road. Soaking wet and stiff from the cold, she returns to the rest area within a couple of minutes, and goes up to the tow truck. "Can you drive me home? It isn't that far and I'll pay you well."

"I'm on duty. You have to move along." He reaches for a clipboard with forms attached. "I'll have to write you up, miss. You can't stay here."

"Why not? There's nothing here."

"That's because I'm doing my job keeping it clear." The man starts the truck's engine and gets out of the cab, leaving the engine running. "Step away, miss."

"Look, my husband is certain to come back for me. He was just having a temper tantrum. He gets mad easily, and then gets over it just as easily. I can assure you he will be back. Just let me wait here. I won't get under your feet."

He pulls a lever on the side of the truck and the flatbed lowers and inclines. He unhooks heavy chains.

"What...who are you?" Her voice is rigid with fear. "What are you going to do?"

"My job, miss."

"But the Municipal code on that sign over there says I'm allowed to park here for eight hours. Of course, I'm not a car but what difference does it make? I take up much less room and have been here for less than an hour." She tries hard to sound in control but her voice trembles and gives her away. "You're the one breaking the law."

"If you have witnesses, you can take me to court, miss."

He wraps a heavy chain around her quaking body, hooks it to a winch that pulls her onto the flatbed. "Your husband can pick you up at the impound yard. It'll cost him a hundred if he gets there before midnight, or there'll be charges over that for each additional day."

Her screams cannot be heard above the engine and rattling chains as the truck drives with all lights flashing through the dark and increasing rain.

PURCHASE GUARANTEED
A One Act play

DAY TIME. A VACUUM CLEANER STANDS IN THE MIDDLE OF A LARGE ROOM. A GARDEN CAN BE SEEN THROUGH FRENCH WINDOWS ON ONE SIDE.

A young woman enters. She walks over to the vacuum cleaner and bends down and scratches her legs. She checks the floor in that area. She leaves the room, returns with a canister of Raid, and starts to spray the floor.

This is all I need. The little blighters are everywhere.

> (She cautiously walks around the vacuum cleaner.)

Unbelievable! They're coming from inside!

> (She sprays the vacuum cleaner then goes to a small desk that has a phone book and telephone. She looks in the book for a moment, and then dials a number.)

Um, yes. This is Liz Mathews. I have an infestation of bugs. No-no, not *me*—my house. The sitting room to be exact. Yes, I tried dealing with them myself but I don't think I was very successful. What do they look like? Bugs, of course. Oh, you're in the area? Good. 5151 Wilson. That's right. Your name? Ed? Thank you.

> (She hangs up the phone and looks around the room. A doorbell rings. She exits and returns with a short chubby man in overalls. He is carrying a clipboard and duffel bag. Liz points to the vacuum cleaner.)

The bugs are coming from there. My husband Joe only bought it yesterday. I've a good mind to return it to the store.

ED

Wouldn't do you much good now.

LIZ

Why not? It's responsible for what's happening.

ED

Well, the bugs have already got off the bus, so to speak. Have you seen any live ones since you sprayed?

LIZ

Yes. The spray hardly helped at all.

ED

Well, let's take a look and see what we have?

> (He takes out a giant magnifying glass from the duffel bag and looks at the bugs scampering on the floor.)

These are not the run of the mill critters I normally see, mam. I've never seen anything like them before. No, indeed. They're beauties.

Beauties? They're filthy smelly creatures. Yuck! I've got the creeps.

(She shivers.)

ED

Come and take a look for yourself. They'll like miniature platypuses but with eight legs. Incredible.

(Ed hands Liz the magnifying glass. She warily holds the glass a couple of inches off the floor and half closes her eyes.)

I don't know what you expect to see, screwing your eyes up like that. Take a look—a good look. This is something really special, I'm telling you.

LIZ

Oh, they are disgusting. They're all hairy and I think they are a bit bigger than before.

ED

Why do you think that?

LIZ

Well, I can see some detail now without the magnifying glass. Before, they were the size of peppercorns. Oh, look over there… more live ones.

ED

Mrs. Mathews, I don't want to alarm you but I need to make a phone call. I think we've got something really special here, and we need to contact the authorities.

LIZ

No-no! Just kill them. My husband will be home from golf soon. He'll be tired, and this is the last thing he'll want to deal with. Please, Ed! Get on with it. Blast them away.

ED

I can't do it, mam. Not now, anyway. I want someone in the know to make that decision.

(He takes out his cell phone and dials a number.)

I'm with Bug-Buster-Buggers, exterminators. I got a call about a beetle infestation, and I'm at the premises now. The perpetrator is an unfamiliar Coleopteran. Before I carry out its demise, I think one of your experts should take a look. 5151 Wilson. Hold on.

(He puts his hand over the cell phone.)

They can come now, mam. They're getting coffee at the 711 around the corner.

LIZ

Oh, if they really have to, but I don't know what my husband will say!

ED
(He talks into the phone again.)

Okay. As soon as you can, buddy.

(He hangs up, and walks around the room, looking at the baseboards, into corners and along the French windows.)

Everything seems to be clean, Mrs. Mathews. Once those guys check, it will only take a couple of minutes for me to deal with everything.

(The doorbell rings. Liz exits the room. She returns followed by a tall lean man with a sparse goatee beard. He is wearing a safari outfit and has a camera and binoculars hanging around his neck.)

LIZ

Here's the bug expert.

PROFESSOR

I'm Professor Lucanidae. As I am currently working with several stag beetle species, it seemed only appropriate to change my name to reflect that. Because my duties change frequently, this helps me to keep on track. Previously, I studied Armadillidium vulgare and took on the name at that time of Professor Roly-poly. It is an excellent system.

(He opens a canvas bag and takes out a pair of glasses.)

Show me what you've got.

ED

I thought this would be a normal run of the mill call, but this creature—well, it's new to me, Professor, and I didn't want to do it in before an expert took a look.

PROFESSOR

Good man. Exactly right.

> (He gets on his hands and knees and slowly makes his way around the floor. He takes out his camera and takes several close-up pictures.)

Most interesting. Yes, indeed. You did the right thing calling in. This is a species we thought we'd never see again.

> (He takes out a notebook and starts to write rapidly.)

This is a thrilling day. We've discovered the Ornithorhynchus-Anatinus Coleoptera…um, that is to say the Duck-Billed Platypus Beetle is alive and well. This particular beetle hasn't been reported seen for many, many years and thought extinct. The world of entomology will be celebrating, I can assure you.

LIZ

Ed, they seem even bigger now. Look at them.

ED

You're right. I can see their bills quite easily. Professor Roly-poly, they've gone from the size of a peppercorn to a kidney bean.

PROFESSOR

Most interesting. I can see for myself they are increasing in size and number quite rapidly. I'll take a couple of specimens with me to the laboratory. I do not want any destroyed. That is direct order. Understood?

LIZ

Of course, we must. If they're not stopped they'll take over the house. Ed, you've got to do something. Do your job, damn it!

ED

She's right, Professor. I have to kill them. There are so many now, they've practically covered the floor.

LIZ

Help, they're climbing up my legs. Oh, they hurt! Get them off... get them off me.

(She rubs at her feet and legs. Blood appears. She jumps up and down in panic.)

(Ed helps her to stand on a chair.)

PROFESSOR

It is so fascinating, Mrs. Mathews. It would appear they have the same defence as the platypus mammal. The spurs on the male hind legs are like hypodermic needles and inject a lethal cocktail. Look.

(He picks up a beetle and holds it out to her.)

Remarkable. Instead of four legs, it has eight. Ouch! They are vicious all right!

(He drops the beetle and sucks at his finger that is now dripping blood.)

ED

I'm going to get my equipment. They've got to be stopped, man!

(He leaves the room. The professor gathers a few specimens into a plastic container.)

PROFESSOR

Come along, now, my beauties. Oh, the world will rejoice over this precious find. We'll track their place of origin to arrive at your home through the vacuum cleaner, Mrs. Mathews.

> (The beetles spike him repeatedly as he tries to push them in to the container. His hands are covered in blood. Liz starts to cry. Ed returns with a tank on his back and holds a hose at the ready. Before he can open the nozzle, the beetles are on him. Panicked, he sprays wildly around the room without any effect.)

Stop man! Pull yourself together.

LIZ

They're taking over. They are growing bigger before our eyes. We're going to die. Joe…oh, Joe, where are you?

> (She sobs uncontrollably.)

PROFESSOR

> (He blows the whistle on a string around his neck.)

Pull yourselves together, both of you. Yes, we have a difficult state of affairs at the moment but hysterics will not help. I suggest you both get on top of the table. You'll be safe there; the wooden legs are too smooth to allow the OACs to ascend.

> (He moves over to Liz, and tries to lift her onto the table. After a short

struggle he is successful. She is
fuming.)

LIZ

You were out of line, professor. It's just as well my husband isn't
here.

PROFESSOR

Come now, Liz…I can call you Liz, can't I? No? All right, Mrs.
Mathews…your buttocks, or, gluteus maximus, as I know them,
are of no interest to me. I've felt and seen a number and, I assure
you, yours…although quite a good sample, are not the best I've
encountered.

(He begins taking more photographs.
He is oblivious of the bugs climbing
up his legs, and one hanging from his
left ear.)

As this species has been found on your private property, you have
to enter into a conservation agreement with the Department of
Fish and Wildlife Services. You will be well compensated if they
secure your property, Mrs. Mathews.

LIZ

Never! This is my home. Ed, help me. I order you to kill every
one or I won't pay you a cent!

PROFESSOR

You'll do no such thing. In the name of science, I arrest you both.

(He takes out a gun from his jacket.)

ED

Oh, yeah? You and whose army may I ask?

PROFESSOR

I don't need an army when I have the law on my side, murderer. This hideous creature, as you call it, is sublime. When the world gets word of this sighting, there will be major celebrations. It is inspirational. A miracle took place somewhere in Eastern Australia or on the Island of Tasmania way-way back in time. The DNA of a platypus was invaded by the DNA of a common beetle. It remained in isolation until it reproduced an offspring carrying the altered gene. Thousands of generations later, a population of OAC was established. Now, you may ask, how did such a species get from there to your vacuum cleaner, Mrs. Mathews? Well, I can't answer that, but I intend to find out.

ED

Put the gun down, professor. Mrs. Mathews and I will do as you say.

PROFESSOR

Now you're being sensible. You must both understand this find must be protected at any cost.

> (He waves the gun around before putting it back into the holster under his jacket. He takes out a cell phone.)

I am going to involve my field team. They will need full access and cooperation, Mrs. Mathews.

> (He walks to the French windows and talks quietly into the cell phone. Ed helps Liz off the table, and they both move slowly towards the door. The professor sees them, and calls out.)

Don't get any dumb ideas. You're wasting your time.

(Ed scoops up a pile of beetles that have now reached the size of Brazil nuts. He runs up to the professor and throws them over him. The professor drops his phone. He covers his face with his hands, and cries out as the beetles attack with their sharp spurs.)

LIZ

Ed, they're on me! Help!

ED

Look out.

(He grabs the tank and turns it on but the hose is blocked by the beetles.)

Oh, Mrs. Mathews. I'm truly sorry. You are a very nice lady but I've got my wife and junior to think about. They count on me so I have to save myself. I have to go.

(He quickly exits through the French windows. The room is quiet except for the sound of thousands of tiny feet scampering over the wood floor.)

LIZ

That new vacuum was no bargain, even with the hundred dollars off.

(She has beetles crawling on her blooded arms and legs. She falls to the floor, and moans with pain.)

(A man wearing a laboratory white coat appears at the French window. He sees the professor on the floor.)

LAB WORKER

Professor Roly-Poly, I'm here for the samples.

(There is no sign of life from the professor and the man walks over to the vacuum cleaner and carefully opens it.)

Come to papa, little ones…oh, goodness, you're not so little, are you? What fun!

(He puts the vacuum cleaner in a large container and seals the opening with industrial tape. The container is heavy and he has difficulty picking it up. He steps over the professor, and drags it through the French windows.)

(A car door slams, and a young man wearing golf attire enters.)

Liz? Honey, I'm home.

(He sees Liz on the floor and rushes over. He pulls her unconscious body to him. He takes out his cell phone.)

JOE

Emergency? I need an ambulance right away. My wife's been attacked. Don't know—got strange wounds all over her. 5151 Wilson. You did? An exterminator, you say? Strange wounds too? What a coincidence. Yes, please hurry.

151

(He hangs up. Liz stirs.)

Take it easy, honey.

LIZ
Joe, thank heavens. I didn't think I'd see you again.

JOE
Don't talk. An ambulance is on its way.

(He hears a groan, and sees the professor on the floor by the French windows.)

Who the hell are you? What's been going on here?

PROFESSOR
Hello, there. Don't be alarmed.

(He lifts his head weakly.)

It's been a rather challenging day but everything is under control. Thanks to your lovely wife, a species thought extinct has come to light again and will be noted in history books.

(His head drops.)

(The house phone rings and the machine picks up.)

This is customer service with your local hardware store. We regret to inform you the deluxe vacuum cleaner you recently purchased has been issued a recall. Do not return the unit to the store. You will be contacted by a professional disposal company. A full refund will be issued. Have a nice day.

UP-UP AND AWAY

The Eureka rose out of a thick cloud bank over Laguna Beach. British pilot Katherine turned to her German mentor, Fritz, and said, "Crickey! Look!"

"Vhat? Vhere?"

"Port side, Fritz!"

He peered through the cockpit window. "Calm down, mein liebe. It's likely another of those Department of Defence secret aircraft."

The craft was pod shaped and covered in graffiti. With a burst of speed, it hovered parallel to the Eureka. Several purple creatures were peering out. One waved its huge hand. A giant yellow megaphone shot out of the craft roof. "'ello luv! We're 'aving a daay at Lagoona Beach. 'Orrible rain in England."

"Cor luv-a-duck, it's got a Liverpool accent!" Katherine reached for the intercom. "Can you hear me? Over."

"Oh, yes." The figure wriggled its elephant-like ears.

"Where did you get that accent?"

"We joost loov the Beatles...we know all their sonngs...went Mersey-side to listen. We live in Loondon, now." The figure gave a smart salute. "I'm Hector."

Fritz reciprocated, clicking his boots. "Your craft is very interesting."

"We nicked it from the London Eye. What a caper, eh? Nice ain't it?" The figure put a six-inch finger to its lips. "I'm talking cockney now. That's wha livin' in London duz ta ya."

"Vhat planet are you from?"

153

"Don't know. We crashed and our ruddy memory disappeared. We remember 'ow to make things go really fast though. That's 'ow we can 'ave a day in Lagoona."

"You look very strange." Katherine said rudely. If she were home, Mummy would have slapped her wrist.

"Blimey, I'm insulted. 'av you seen what's walking around London nowa days?" Hector beckoned another figure forward. "Every family in Britain has a Mum. To fit in proper, we made this our Mum." Singing suddenly erupted from the megaphone. *All you need is love, dada da da....* Hector rocked back and forth in time to the music. "This is our favourite. We fly over cities and play it while people are sleeping."

"But vhy? Vhat's your point?" Fritz asked suspiciously.

"If all you need is love is heard over and over, it might permeate people's subconscious, and change attitudes. We're trying, anyway." Hector beamed, cheekily. "That's a magnificent dirigible you've got, but take it back and 'ave a day at the beach with us."

Fritz and Katherine looked at each other. Should they—could they? Fritz cleared his throat. "Ve could meet you in front of the ice cream parlour at two."

"Mum wants to look at art galleries. Two would be blooming perfick!" Hector waved. "See you soon then." The megaphone withdrew; following a loud rumbling, the pod sped off.

Static spluttered on the radio; a monotone voice asked, "What is your position, Eureka One?"

Katherine cut the connection. "Pinch me, Fritz, Is this a dream? Ouch!! I didn't mean really pinch me!"

Fritz laughed giddily. "Vhatever it is, mein captain, I'm returning this bag of vind to Long Beach NOW. I've got a date with Mum at two! Von't you join us, Fraulein?"

"A pleasure, mein Professor!"

CPSIA information can be obtained
at www.ICGtesting.com
Printed in the USA
BVHW031721280519
549479BV00004B/25/P